INTERVIEW

MISTAKES

You Don't Even

KNOW

YOU'RE MAKING

Bill Cole, MS, MA

Silicon Valley, California

ABP

Special discounts on bulk quantities of Albert-Brownson Publishing books are available to corp-orations, professional associations, governmental entities and other organizations to use as sales promotions, premiums and training resources. Private imprints may also be arranged. For details, contact Albert-Brownson Publishing, 19925 Stevens Creek Blvd., Suite 100, Cupertino, CA 95014-2358, 408-725-7191.

International rights and foreign translations available only through negotiation with Albert-Brownson Publishing.

Library of Congress Cataloging In Publication Data

Cole, William B. Interview Mistakes You Don't Even Know You're Making.

Reference 2. Communication 3. Business I. Title ISBN: 1-931825-14-9 $19.95

DISCLAIMER

This book was written to provide information on the Do's and Dont's of career-building strategies and tactics about the world of interviewing.

The author and publisher are not engaged in rendering legal, medical, accounting, psychological, career, counseling or other professional advice or services. If assistance of this type is sought, the services of the appropriate, competent professional should be consulted.

This publication does not contain all the available information about interviewing available to potential or current interviewees. It instead attempts to supplement, support and add to existing texts and other information sources. The reader is encouraged to consult all pertinent available material, in all published forms, and adapt and customize the material to their specific career and interviewing needs.

Interviewing is not a simple endeavor. This book does not purport or suggest that interviewing is easy to do, nor easy to succeed in. Interviewing is a challenging undertaking, one that has risks, as any other endeavor has. Anyone attempting to interview should expect to invest considerable time, money and effort to reach a level of success.

1

ACKNOWLEDGEMENTS

I would like to acknowledge the most important person who helped in the writing and production of this book. That would be my wonderful wife, Amy Lao. I could not have written this book without her advice, insight and unfailing support. I am forever indebted to her.

I also owe a special thanks to my clients who teach me as I teach them.

Bill Cole, MS, MA

DEDICATION

This book is dedicated to all the job seekers in the world who want to give an excellent interview and who want to avoid the many hidden pitfalls in a job hunt.

WHAT IS NOT IN THIS BOOK

This book shows you how to know the difference between the Do's and Dont's of the job hunt and interview game. It's not enough for someone to tell you to be on your best behavior, to be professional, or to have good manners. That's because everyone has different definitions of these. These behaviors also vary according to the profession, the country and the position you are seeking.

To do well in the interview game you need a huge, multifaceted skill set. This book focuses on those career strategies and interview tactics that help you navigate this undertaking. This book covers the nuts and bolts of what you need to know in terms of career strategies, business skills, interview skills, people skills and many other topics.

In my next book I may cover some of these topics:

1. Contracts

2. Career advice

3. Branding

4. Dealing with bad bosses

5. Handling toxic co-workers

6. Self-sabotage in a career

7. Politics in corporate life
8. Dealing with HR people
9. Working in teams
10. Transitioning from corporate life to your own business
11. How to stay motivated when you are out of work
12. Dealing with hostile interviewers

What additional topics would you like to see me cover? Drop me a line and let me know.

HOW TO USE THIS BOOK

I wrote this book so you can use it as your personal guide to the world of interviewing.

This book doesn't need to be read in a linear manner from start to finish. Feel free to jump around and explore areas that you need right now. Whenever you have a question on a particular topic, go to that chapter and dig in. Make notes after your interviews of trouble areas that came up and see if those are covered in each chapter. If not, send me an email and I'd be happy to discuss it with you.

The book is divided into 16 chapters. For example, I describe mistakes people make in working with recruiters and headhunters so if you work with recruiters or headhunters this chapter will give you insights into how to maximize your time with them. As you read each mistake, think of the reaction a recruiter or headhunter would have to it. Your goal is to work together smoothly so you both get a win-win. Knowing these mistakes, and then avoiding them is a great start.

There are chapters on job offer negotiations, and one with resumes, CV's and cover letters. There are specialty chapters on running your job hunt campaign and avoiding mistakes about your resume and other written materials.

Then I break down the actual interview in terms of time. I have sections ranging from before, during and after the interview. Many people make lots of mistakes at the start and end of their interview, so I have those lists for you. I break down errors in the actual interview into verbal and behavioral mistakes.

Then I have mistakes that are made with dining interviews, and with those specialized questions known as "behavioral interview questions". These are the questions an interviewer begins by saying, "Tell me about a time when you...". Most people don't like answering these too much.

The lists are designed to be very fast reading. They are visually easy to scan quickly. Each item makes immediate sense. You will know in an instant what you have been doing wrong. You'll know exactly what NOT to do. When you read each "What not to do" it will be obvious WHY that behavior or verbalization is wrong.

As successful people will tell you, it's not what you have to avoid doing, it's

what you don't know that you don't know that can really hurt you. This book is your e-ticket ride to freedom. It will make you aware.

Finally, I saved the best for last. Or maybe I should say I saved the "worst" for last. Here in the final chapter I show you what some unfortunate souls have said and done in their interviews that resulted in, ahem, less than desirable outcomes. I call this the ultimate list of self-sabotaging interview mistakes. You could call this final chapter the Super Bowl of interview mistakes. These are truly world-class blunders. Top-level gaffs. These are industrial-strength boo-boos.

I hope you enjoy reading about all that could go wrong in an interview. I want you to laugh and learn your way to job success!

INTRODUCTION

This book came about because for years my clients would always ask me how they should "behave" in an interview. They asked me what they should avoid doing. They asked me what the interviewer would see as bad behavior. They asked me what successful interviewees do. And what they don't do. In short, they wanted to know everything about how to think, how to act and how to feel in an interview situation. This book covers every conceivable thing you could say or do in an interview.

Most interview skills books only cover what takes place in the actual interview room. You will see that this book covers the full range of situations and behaviors you need to succeed in all those situations, from before the interview to after the interview. There are specialty chapters on creating and managing a cohesive job hunt campaign, working with recruiters and being smart about your resume and other written materials.

Awareness is the master skill. If you have it, all things are possible. If you don't have it, almost nothing is possible. This book is all about awareness. It's about being aware of what CAN happen in an interview situation, comparing that to what you actually DO in such a situation, and knowing how to REGULATE yourself so you act the way you

PREFER in that situation. Awareness is your best friend. You need it. And this book gives it to you.

As you read through these interview scenarios and situations you may be thinking, "I would never do that! That's nutty behavior. It's rude or just plain dumb!". And you'd be right. Yet people do those things. Some of the situations you'll see here are very, very basic. But for younger folks and newbies to the interview game, how do they know that? How do they know what to do and what to avoid? Read this book, that's how.

If you are a veteran of the interview wars, you'll find this book highly useful, on multiple levels. You'll first confirm that you indeed already avoid many of these self-sabotaging behaviors, and know that you are on the right track. You'll get a kick out of reading what some people actually think is acceptable behavior. Remember how many mistakes you made early in your career?

The most important thing you'll get from this book are the subtle, golden nuggets of insight that show you what you have been doing wrong all this time. Why you have not been getting that pass to the next round of the interview process. Why you have been feeling stuck. I can't tell you how many people contact me and say, "What am I doing wrong in my interviews? I have no idea!!". This book removes that frustration.

A major feature you will see running through this book is about how well you communicate in an interview. Interviewers want to know if you can be agreeable as you disagree. Can you be diplomatic? Tactful? Are you perceived as a know-it-all? The very bottom line every interviewer has in their mind is this: "If this person is this disagreeable now, when they should be on their very best behavior, how will they be once they are actually on the job?" Your task in the interview is to get a green light in the mind of the interviewer by passing the likeability test.

On the Internet we all see articles that describe the top five or ten or 20 worst mistakes you can make in an interview. The largest number I have ever seen was 50. This book is the largest compendium of interview mistakes ever assembled—1765. You will never find a larger collection of interview mistakes anywhere.

Yes, sometimes I have a life.

TABLE OF CONTENTS

"   **"**

THE INTERVIEW GAME

"You moon the wrong person at an office party and suddenly you're not 'professional' anymore."

Jeff Foxworthy

"Most bosses never lift a finger at work, unless it's to point out something you did wrong."

Alfred E. Neuman

"You can make your own breaks in your career. Don't break your career by giving a bad interview."

Bill Cole, MS, MA

DO YOU KNOW HOW MANY INTERVIEW MISTAKES YOU ARE MAKING?

As a long-time interview coach, I hear about many interviewing blunders that happen on both sides of the interview table. Interviewers themselves are not known for being perfect. But if you are seeking to create rapport and a positive image with the interviewer, there are many potential pitfalls that lurk about in an interview situation. There are plenty of rapport killers and social faux pas that can derail an interview. As the saying goes, "What you don't know is what can truly hurt you".

This book is designed to help you become aware of the pitfalls that many interviewees fall victim to. As you become familiar with these, you can watch for them in your own behavior. If you don't know what they are, you can't be alert to them.

I know that going to interviews is one of your greatest pleasures in life. I know you wake up the day of an interview and breathlessly count the minutes before you can traipse into the hiring manager's office to lay your soul bare to this total stranger. Well, I think you can already tell we are going to have some fun with a very serious subject--finding and getting a job.

I've heard well-meaning people say to interviewees, "Just go in there, be yourself, be professional, and you will come across well". Good advice, but I wish it were that simple. Anyone can tell you to be on your best behavior, show good manners, and be attuned to other people socially, but these days in particular, many people just don't know what these social rules, guidelines and conventions are. It sometimes seems like good manners have gone out the window. They don't know the Do's and Dont's of well-mannered behavior. It's not enough for someone to tell you to "Be professional" because everyone has a different definition of the word "professional". We need to define and describe these behaviors. I do that in this book.

The Purpose Of An Interview

Many interviewers will tell you that they have only three things they seek to determine in an interview.

1. Can you do the job?

2. Do you want to do the job?

3. Can we get along with you?

In the first requirement, your task is to show how well your background is the perfect fit for what their position entails. That is called "showing the fit".

In the second aspect, the interviewer needs to know if you are truly motivated and excited about the position. That may sound odd to you, but many otherwise well-qualified people don't fulfill that requirement. They are over-qualified (so they may well be bored, perform substandard work and seek another job soon), they are using this job as a stepping-stone to another job, or they are practicing their interview skills. Yes, people go to interviews for jobs they don't want to get experience in doing interviews. (Don't tell that to the interviewer!)

In the third task, the interviewer is sizing you up by using the snowed-in-the-airport test. They think, if I was on a business trip with this person, and we got snowed in at some airport, could I hang out with them for a few days, or would they drive me crazy? Basically here they want to know if you fit the culture of their organization. Can they get along with you? Do you play well with others? Are you a team player or a quirky, unhappy, irritating lone wolf?

It Won't Get Any Better

Interviewers know a very powerful truth about human behavior. The behavior they see you exhibit in an interview is the BEST behavior they will ever see from you. That's because everyone is on their very best behavior in an interview. They want to put their best foot forward. They want to make that great first impression. The interviewer knows that it will never get any better than what they see and hear you do NOW. Feeling the pressure?

The interviewer is listening and observing. When they see, hear or sense something they view as an issue in you, they make a mental or written note of it. If there are enough of these issues, you have crossed the line and the interviewer will reject you. But they will RARELY TELL YOU about these issues. You think the interview is moving along nicely, but the interviewer has other ideas. This is called a blind spot. Every human has blind spots. These are the unknown behaviors that only others can see in us. No one is immune from this. This book's main purpose is to help you see the behaviors in yourself that others see. Then you can control, adjust, change or stop these behaviors, come across better to interviewers, and make a great impression. Sounds simple, right?

Interviewers know that it is rare for anyone's behavior to improve after the interview process since everyone is on their best behavior, so they use your behavior in the interview as a baseline measure. If you display poor manners there, an interviewer will figure, day to day, that you may likely be less desirable to be around. So if your behavior is borderline, unprofessional or odd in the interview, many interviewers will not take a chance on you.

These are the danger behaviors you need to become aware of if you hope to give an interview that does not become unconsciously self-sabotaged. We call these blunders, gaffs, errors, mistakes or bad manners. The interviewer sees them as things that rub them the wrong way, that would bother other people, and that would get in the way of smooth organizational functioning. Fair or not, interviewers will always make inferences and judgments about your behavior, based on this small sample of time in an interview.

How Executives Derail Themselves

A book has been written about this blind spot phenomenon, describing the low awareness of bad behaviors failed CEO's possess. In the book *Why CEOs Fail*: *The 11 Behaviors That Can Derail Your Climb to the Top and How to Manage Them,* David L. Dotlich and Peter C. Cairo describe the eleven most common characteristics of derailed top executives.

Here they are:

1. **Arrogance:** You think you are better than other people, and that you don't have very much to learn.

2. **Melodrama:** You love being In the spotlight and the one everyone watches.

3. **Volatility:** You are emotionally labile. Your mood swings define you.

4. **Excessive Caution:** Fear runs your life, and you become paralyzed with indecision.

5. **Habitual Distrust:** You delegate poorly, and find it hard to bond with people.

6. **Aloofness:** You are an island unto yourself, and don't really seem to need other people.

7. **Mischievousness:** You believe that rules are made to be broken.

8. **Eccentricity:** You are a non-conformist or have quirky habits and behaviors.

9. **Passive Resistance:** You are clever, tricky and insincere and don't say what you mean.

10. **Perfectionism:** You see the world in either-or terms, drive yourself mercilessly, and have astronomical, unrealistic standards.

11. **Eagerness to Please:** You are very needy for approval.

I'm sure you have known people with some of these unfortunate traits. They don't get along well with others, cause problems, and often become a liability for the organization. These are the very behaviors interviewers are watching for. Interviewers want you to succeed, buy they are also gatekeepers for their organization. They must weed out people who won't fit. Your job is to come across as a person who WILL fit.

Image Management

The successful job candidate has smart and polished social interviewing etiquette. They are aware of themselves, and of others. Most critically, they are aware of how they come across to others. They know how others perceive them. If you are self-aware, you can control the image you project to the world. This is called image management. Think of an actor who portrays a certain role so well that you almost forget they are acting.

Remember, it's not the message you send that is important. It's the message that is received that counts. If you believe you are a debonair, smooth, modern, stylistic operator, yet the interviewer sees you to be a clumsy, self-centered oaf, you can guess which image will stick. The image you portray to the interviewer is critical. You must be aware of that image and manage that image intentionally.

In addition to of course having high quality answers in the interview, you must look and sound like you fit their organization. This is what image management is all about.

25

How Do Interviewers React?

If you looked through the table of contents you can see that there is a huge number of mistakes people make in the interview game. Your task is to become aware of these errors, and to avoid them. One way to do this is to read the behavior as it is described, and to use this list below to interpret that behavior. You can ask yourself, "If I were the interviewer, and I heard or saw the interviewee do that, what would I think? How would I feel? How would I react? Would I want that person on my team?" That is exactly what the interviewer's thought process is.

Who Makes These Mistakes?

I have gathered these mistakes from a wide range of sources such as clients who initially come to me after having failed their interviews, recruiters, hiring managers, and in speaking with other executive coaches. These mistakes are made in entry-level jobs to the executive suite, from every industry, for blue-collar, white-collar and academics, and from young people to seniors. Interviewees in every conceivable type of profession make these mistakes.

The mistakes covered in this book are representative across a range from people starting their careers to folks who are mid-career and beyond.

Younger people starting out in the work world often don't know what is considered acceptable behavior in the workplace. They will often make very basic mistakes in their interviews. After a few years of working, you would think that everyone would know what good and bad behavior is, but not really. You'd be surprised. In my coaching practice I see people across every age group, and every industry, and even senior folks making mistakes that can hurt them. If you are mid-career or beyond, and you read some obvious mistakes here, realize that young and inexperienced people often make these mistakes. You can skip past these to the "more sophisticated mistakes". Makes you feel better, doesn't it?

Don't Disqualify Yourself

Some interviewees almost directly say that they are not a good fit for the job. They doubt themselves, they put themselves down and they don't know how to show they can do the job. They almost testify against themselves. I want you to do the interview behavior basics well so you don't disqualify yourself. The interviewers are looking for ways to disqualify people. Don't give them any ammunition.

The trick is to limit these mistakes to an absolute minimum. This is known as reducing your unforced errors. Stop doing simple things that get you in trouble with the interviewer.

Stop shooting yourself in the foot. Stop doing yourself in. Stop the self-sabotage.

Self-sabotaging behaviors are those you exhibit to the interviewer where you don't even know you're hurting yourself. These blind spots cause damage, and you don't even know it. They can be lethal, job-killing mistakes. But once you know these pet peeves that bug interviewers, you will have the proper etiquette, and you'll stop taking yourself out of the game. I want you to become aware of these deal-breakers so you can make better choices, act with diplomacy and tact, sell yourself, and get the job.

How Interviewers React To Interviewee Behavior

Read each item on the various lists in the book and have this checklist handy as a way to gauge your reaction to that item. Your reaction would probably mirror that of the interviewer. For example, you can see here the example of the interviewee acting in a micro-managing and over-controlling manner:

Interviewee's Alienating Behavior: The interviewee dominates and takes the interview over by asking too many questions, directing the interview's focus, and by generally being controlling.

Why This Is A Problem: This the interviewer's turf and they are in charge of the meeting so they don't take kindly to some stranger coming in and trying to take over. They will naturally assume that if you are this controlling and aggressive in the very first meeting, before you are hired, you will be far worse once you are hired. The Result: The interviewee very likely will not get another interview or an offer.

You can see how an interviewer would naturally react negatively to such a controlling person. This interviewee did not exhibit restraint, deference, patience or pay attention to rapport. And they paid the price. Very likely this unbridled impetuousness of the interviewee is a blind spot.

Let's take a look at how interviewers think about and react to the behaviors and answers of interviewees.

Issues About Rapport And Manners

You can see the various escalating levels of concern an interviewer would have with an interviewee's questionable behavior.

1. This shows the interviewee has a negative or defeatist attitude.

2. This behavior is not creating rapport between us. He's cold and distant.

3.   This behavior is irritating and makes me feel uncomfortable. If I'm having a negative reaction to this person, I can assume that others will also.

4.   He seems like he's got something to hide. He's secretive and evasive. He's avoiding some of my questions. He changes the subject for no reason.

5.   They clearly are showing that they are unable to "play well with others". This guy is simply displaying bad manners, and his behavior shows he is self-centered and only thinks of himself.

6.   This shows they are too aggressive, and that they trample on the rights of others. They're clumsy socially, not sensitive to the feelings of others and not respectful of others.

7.   This shows he doesn't have the emotional maturity for the position. This shows they are not trustworthy or reliable.

8.   This shows they are not taking the interview seriously. His behavior is even insulting.

9. This behavior is way over the top, and any organization would view this interviewee as a dangerous liability. I need to seriously question this interviewee's judgment.

Issues About Fit For The Position Or Organization

You can see the various concerns an interviewer would have with an interviewee's answers and fit for the position.

1. Their answers are not on target, weak, short, rambling, or disorganized.

2. This shows they don't understand how our business operates.

3. This shows they are inexperienced, and not what we are seeking.

Always Act In Your Own Best Interests

Remember that self-sabotage is unconscious. You don't know you are doing it. But this book helps you avoid that. I really want you to understand this preceding list well and think it through relative to how you think, react emotionally, and act in an interview. If you don't, your natural, yet incorrect reactions may tend to appear, and you may unknowingly derail your chances at creating an alliance with your interviewer. You need to get along with the interviewer. You can't alienate this person, because, after all, they hold the power to either block you and reject you, or pass you through to your next career move. Make the best decisions possible for yourself and be likeable, smooth and non-abrasive.

" **"**

THE INTERVIEW GAME

"The best way to appreciate your job is to imagine yourself without one."

Oscar Wilde

"Oh, you hate your job? Why didn't you say so? There's a support group for that. It's called EVERYBODY, and they meet at the bar."

Drew Carey

"The essential and ongoing task of a job interview is to demonstrate how well your capabilities fit into the requirements of the position being offered."

Bill Cole, MS, MA

141 MISTAKES YOU MAKE IN JOB HUNT STRATEGIES

The care and feeding of a career takes a lot of time. The same with a job hunt. Unfortunately, many people just don't put in the quality time required for these tasks, and they pay the price. This chapter gives you insights into the many ways people ruin their job hunt (and careers) so you can avoid that heartache. I really want you to succeed, and knowing these potential pitfalls is a great start. It's a jungle out there, but you can be the King of that jungle if you know what to do. Good luck!

1. You don't really have a strategy. Instead, you just send things out by "feel".

2. You are seeking a full-time job with part-time time and effort.

3. You don't follow precise or special requests of the employer in completing their paperwork.

4. You use unusual job titles or key words in the company's APS (Applicant

Tracking System) and therefore miss out on targeted queries.

5. You don't know that one excellent in-person meeting can be as effective as hundreds of emails or LinkedIn connections.

6. You use only the big-name job posting websites and ignore the smaller, niche-oriented websites.

7. You network aggressively, yet you forget to provide value for others, and are mainly interested in what's in it for you, so people don't reciprocate.

8. Instead of making your job hunt into a do-it-yourself project, you expect outplacement counselors, or recruiters to do it all for you.

9. You disclose confidential details to a potential employer, and they correctly view you as untrustworthy.

10. You work on your job hunt tasks "when you have time", not according to a schedule.

11. You thought you had such a secure job, you don't have a vibrant network in place because you didn't think you needed this support system.

12. You spend too much time promoting yourself on-line with blogs, social media and other digital time traps.

13. You use the same cover letter for each company you contact.

14. You are random and don't keep records in your networking. You don't treat it as a job.

15. You don't make it clear why you want the position.

16. If a job description does not match your capabilities to a T, you give up and don't apply.

17. You tell the recruiter you need a job and that you'll take anything he can find for you.

18. You use the heart of the day for Internet searches when you should reserve this for before 7:30 a.m. and after 7:30 p.m., and instead use the

day to get out and meet people.

19.   You write your LinkedIn profile in the third person.

20.   Your LinkedIn profile is a mix of first person and third person.

21.   You include your nickname on a resume.

22.   You confuse LinkedIn with social media, and post personal content.

23.   You make your LinkedIn content showing you still have a job so you look more desirable to employers, but then you have to explain this discrepancy at the interview.

24.   You have not articulated your brand or special sauce enough to be able to position yourself properly to companies.

25.   As an executive of many years, you never had a resume to speak of because you had jobs coming at you all the time. But now, when jobs are tighter, you have no real job history documentation.

26. You don't do very much research on the company and when asked what you know about them, you give a very thin answer.

27. You think you can make up for a lack of experience with just passion and great salesmanship.

28. Many employers use specific phrases in their job postings, and you ignore these and apply anyhow, and are bypassed by the ATS system.

29. You look for "openings" instead of "opportunities".

30. You get discouraged quickly in networking, not realizing that it is a distance run, not a sprint.

31. If you are an executive, or well-known in your industry, you may act like your "record speaks for itself".

32. You love to apply to job boards, even though fewer than 10% of jobs at the executive level are landed through job boards.

33. You did a job search many years ago, and you think using the same strategies this time will be fine. You don't agree with the saying, "If you do what you've always done, you'll get what you've always got".

34. You've set goals for your job search, but no benchmarks and metrics so you can truly measure your progress.

35. You haven't clarified your values, goals and desires for your next job.

36. You are either far too specific about the job you want, or you'll take the first thing that comes along.

37. You don't know the buzz words in your industry or niche.

38. You don't get any insider information about the company at all before you interview.

39. You show up to the interview looking 100% different from your on-line photos.

40. You don't secure a "champion" inside the company to guide you and to use

as a reference.

41. You don't know about using websites like PayScale.com to do compensation benchmarking.

42. You have a reactive, not proactive approach to your job hunt.

43. You figure the more the merrier and apply to as many jobs as you possibly can.

44. You focus only on expanding your network with new people, and you neglect people you've known a long time.

45. You don't know about the 'hidden job market', sometimes called opportunistic hiring, and miss out on being able to create your own job description.

46. You don't have keyword-focused and accomplishment-based summary, headline and job descriptions on your LinkedIn page.

47. You don't ask for recommendations to use on LinkedIn.

48. You have not adequately explained gaps in your employment.

49. Even though you could take some time off and decompress from the stress of an abusive boss, you jump right into a job search and interview while you're still emotionally distraught, and interview badly.

50. You use a single job hunt strategy instead of a multi-pronged one.

51. You attempt to turn an informational interview into a job interview.

52. You keep your job search to yourself and don't tell all your friends so they can advocate for you.

53. You put you career ahead of your personal life and now you regret it.

54. At the end of an informational interview you don't ask, "Is there anyone else with whom you recommend I speak?

55. You connect with a new person on LinkedIn and immediately pitch them for a favor or try to sell them a product

or service.

56. You forget that no matter how high the unemployment rate gets, you only need ONE job.

57. You send unsolicited resumes to people after you meet them and ask them to "send it around" to see what comes up, ruining what little rapport you've developed with them.

58. You some across as a stalker on LinkedIn, because LinkedIn users can see people who visited their profile. If you visit a certain recruiter or hiring manager too often, that makes them uncomfortable.

59. In your career, you assume that what got you to level one will get you to level two. IQ is a good start, but EQ (Emotional Intelligence) is what makes you in the rest of your career.

60. You don't realize that once you get a job and you are on the ground, other opportunities open up, ones you could not see from the confines of your home office.

61. You think your job security will last forever, so you don't make contingency plans for your next job...now.

62. You see a job failure as permanent, rather as a stepping stone to the next good thing.

63. You work primarily for money, rather than growth.

64. You become frustrated because you don't qualify companies well enough to realize the fit is not good, yet you apply for their jobs anyhow.

65. You don't use websites like the muse.com or glassdoor.com.

66. You include generic, menial tasks rather than accomplishments.

67. You use graphics and tables that may confuse an ATS.

68. You don't set goals with your networking, such as meeting three new people per week.

69. You apply to multiple jobs at the same company, sending the message that you really don't have focus, and / or you don't know what you want.

70. On LinkedIn your resume and profile are contradictory.

71. Instead of following the company's job application procedure, you try to bypass it by asking for special favors.

72. You only apply for positions that represent your "dream job".

73. You overlook significant negatives about a job because it could be your "dream job".

74. You have gradually allowed your skills to become out of date.

75. You allow a recruiter to alter your resume without your permission, and thereby misrepresent you.

76. Your resume has quirky or overly-clever and unusual job titles, and employers can't figure you out or don't want to take a chance on doing so.

77. It is estimated that 50-60% of resumes and cover letters have typos, but you don't proofread very carefully so you can stand out in the better percentage.

78. You don't know how to figure out what a company needs, and give it to them, even if they don't tell you what it is.

79. You talk money with a company before you have clearly established your full value to them.

80. You don't know if you should choose a job or an industry as a career path. Choosing a job gives you expertise. Choosing an industry makes you an expert.

81. You've burned bridges in your career because at the time, that felt good, or it just happened.

82. You think the grass is always greener at other companies, and that makes you unappreciative of what you currently have.

83. You job hunt while working at your job, and your employer discovers this.

84. Your pride won't let you tell your friends and associates you need their help in your job hunt.

85. You create and send emails in a hurry, and make many errors you are never aware of.

86. You don't use a resume website, and you don't promote it properly.

87. You either don't use LinkedIn, or you have a poor profile.

88. You don't have a LinkedIn banner headline that summarizes who you are.

89. Your LinkedIn photo is too small, too casual, too old, or too "something" that immediately marks you as undesirable.

90. You don't use the LinkedIn link where you can see what headline other people in your industry are using.

91. You restrict your networking to people you've met recently.

92. You prejudge people in your network based on how you think they can help you or not, and thereby shrink your

network.

93. In a rush to be first in applying to a new job post, you hurry everything up and you are indeed first or one of the early ones, but in your haste you have made many mistakes, and your application is dismissed out of hand.

94. You rely on spell-check to handle your resume, and you don't proofread it before you hit "send".

95. You don't tap your association and alumni networks.

96. You read a job description and immediately see the problems with it, instead of the possibilities.

97. You don't volunteer, do pro bono work, or stay busy and in circulation.

98. You tell your entire life story in your cover letter and resume.

99. You ignore or discount all temporary positions, and only go for full-time jobs.

100. You submit your resume to multiple recruiters at once.

101. You've been on cruise control for a long time and you don't yet have the winner's mind set built up yet.

102. Part of your strategy is to go for the "sympathy vote" by describing how many problems you've had lately. You believe an employer wants to hear about such bad luck and hardships.

103. You conduct your job campaign from your home, and rarely get out and circulate.

104. You rely on email as your only contact method, and don't realize that email can be very unreliable.

105. You are not proactive by taking a course, getting a certificate, reading books, or getting coaching on your areas of deficiency so you can present yourself as the complete package to companies.

106. Your LinkedIn photo makes you look severe, cold, or downright mean.

107. You don't keep your resume updated, and you don't stay attuned with the job market, because you already have a job.

108. You think you can craft and execute your entire job search all by yourself, with no help from friends, a coach, a consultant or colleagues.

109. As your job hunt lengthens, without success, you become cynical and negative and that attitude comes through in your written materials, on the phone, and on person.

110. You are too hung up on titles and lose some very good jobs because you were too rigid.

111. You don't volunteer so you can use that as a resume item.

112. You take consulting jobs, but leave consulting off your resume, or just refer to them as "odd-jobs" or free-lancing, instead of naming your company and making it sound substantial.

113. You don't know how to portray yourself as a problem solver for the companies

that need you.

114. You post your resume and are not careful to protect your privacy and data.

115. You apply to jobs where you do not meet the minimum requirements.

116. You don't reciprocate when fellow job hunters or colleagues help you. Then they lose their interest in enthusiastically helping further.

117. You have unrealistic salary expectations.

118. You don't see that your wonderful skill set from one area of work, volunteerism or life would fit nicely into a new area of work you'd like to enter.

119. You use your work email on your resume.

120. You don't do a Google or LinkedIn search on the people you will meet at the company for an interview.

121. If rejected for a position, you give up, you don't send a thank you note anyhow, and you lose a potentially valuable contact for the future.

122. You accept a counter-offer from your current company, marking you as a short-timer, and one who is not very loyal.

123. You have never checked yourself out on the Internet to see what potentially damaging material might be there.

124. You continue to post potentially damaging material on social media, even though you know employers scan for that content.

125. You think that as long as you accurately describe what your capabilities are, some company will eagerly recognize your value and contact you.

126. You don't pre-screen your references, and when the company calls them, they are surprised, unhappy you didn't ask permission, and only give a luke-warm appraisal of you.

127. Your written materials are not pleasing to the eye, and are difficult to read.

128. You don't know how to tactfully be top of mind with the hiring manager when it comes to checking in with them. Instead, you are perceived as a

nagging pest.

129. You don't use proper formatting in your written materials, and send out huge blocks of text that are not inviting to read.

130. You are too picky about trying to find the "perfect job".

131. You rely on advertised job openings for job leads.

132. You're an introvert so you avoid speaking with people if at all possible.

133. You post on job boards and wait for companies to respond.

134. You don't like to network, so you don't.

135. You have one all-purpose resume you send out regardless of the position, industry or company.

136. You don't know about or use keywords in your resume.

137. You take a passive approach and wait for the phone to ring instead of making

calls.

138. You repeat your resume in your cover letter.

139. You sound "salesy and aggressive" in your written materials.

140. You don't get back to the hiring manager in a timely manner.

141. You don't keep your options open and assume you will get a certain job, and then stop interviewing elsewhere until you hear a final decision from the one company.

65 MISTAKES YOU MAKE IN DEALING WITH RECRUITERS AND HEADHUNTERS

The term headhunter sounds so ominous, doesn't it? Did this term originate with warlike tribes of people? Come to think of it, interviewers can seem like warlike tribes of people. Oh, well. At least recruiter has the connotation of welcoming people into some sort of club or something. Both of these professions seem very, very mysterious. Few people know what they actually do. I've met a few of them who don't really know themselves. But they are very valuable to you as a job seeker. I suggest you scrutinize this list of common mistakes and stay on your best behavior with both the recruiters and headhunters.

1.   You treat a recruiter like they work for you.

2.   You treat an interview with a recruiter as if it isn't a "real" interview.

3.   You portray yourself as being the perfect candidate so the recruiter can sell you easier. But when the

interviewer meets you, they see you puffed up your background.

4. You are not very coachable, and you fail to take action on the recruiter's suggestions.

5. You don't get the recruiter the materials they need to sell you.

6. You undermine the recruiter by going around them and communicating directly with the hiring organization, on your terms and schedule.

7. You use multiple email addresses to communicate with the recruiter, confusing them.

8. You use your spouse's email with the recruiter.

9. You tell the recruiter you are currently employed, when you are not, in order to look better to a potential employer.

10. You lie to the recruiter about why you were fired.

11. You tell the recruiter you resigned, when in actuality you were fired.

12. You brag that you were a part of the 'leadership' team that was responsible for a particular initiative, but you were just on the fringes.

13. You tell the recruiter your overall GPA was a 3.3, yet your major GPA was only a 1.9.

14. You use the recruiter as your personal therapist.

15. You choose the wrong recruiter, one who does not specialize in your field.

16. You get concerned about the model (contingency or retained) the recruiter uses, and that distracts you and them.

17. You become a pest to the recruiter, and use up too much of their time.

18. You toy with the recruiter, and don't make a real commitment to see the process through.

19. You second-guess the recruiter, and tell them how to do their job.

20. You fail to show gratitude to the recruiter, thinking instead since they get paid by the company, you can just slip into the background.

21. You sever ties with the recruiter after you get the job, instead of keeping them as a valuable networking tool.

22. You get upset with the recruiter because you feel they are not telling you everything about what the company wants.

23. You try to use the recruiter as a career counselor.

24. You think the recruiter makes the decision about whether you get the job or not.

25. You trust the recruiter too much, rely on them too much, and expect them to do your work for you.

26. You don't do your due diligence before you hire a recruiter.

27. You decide to work with a generalist recruiter, rather than a specialist.

28. You play it close to the vest with the recruiter rather than being open about what you want, and about your background.

29. You expect the recruiter to do your job hunt work for you.

30. You breach confidentiality with the recruiter.

31. You don't follow up with the recruiter after your interviews.

32. You discount the advice given to you by the recruiter.

33. You put your profile picture on your resume, and the recruiter can't sell you as easily.

34. You change your salary requirements late in the game.

35. You apply for every job possible, instead of being selective, and you look

lazy and desperate.

36. Your resume has tasks and roles, not accomplishments, and they can't sell you effectively.

37. You claim you are a jack of all trades and can do whatever a company needs.

38. You don't delimit your search. You don't tell the recruiter the jobs you DON'T want.

39. You throw last-minute changes at the recruiter, requiring them to change how they sell you.

40. You can't describe how you excelled at your job to set yourself apart from all the other candidates.

41. You call headhunters recruiters and vice–versa, and they're not the same.

42. You treat the recruiter as a career coach, and want them to explore with you what direction you should go.

43. You don't research recruiters before you call or email them.

44. You approach your time with a recruiter or headhunter transactionally rather than as relationship development.

45. You have a mismatch between your elevator pitch, your LinkedIn profile and your resume.

46. You don't accept coaching from the recruiter or headhunter very willingly.

47. You don't trust the judgment of the recruiter or headhunter, even though they see hundreds if not thousands of resumes a year.

48. You don't have your profession listed in your LinkedIn headline so your invitations tell your target audience what you do for a living.

49. You don't have a story to tell, but instead, just a bunch of facts.

50. You tout your technical skills and tell the recruiter or headhunter your social skills are fine, but they're not.

51. You talk money immediately with the recruiter or headhunter.

52. You say that the answer to one of their questions is on your resume.

53. You talk about why you need the job, instead of talking about why you are the right person for the job.

54. Once you get a job, you don't respond to the recruiter or headhunter any longer.

55. You don't keep your eyes and ears open for opportunities and candidates and share that information with the recruiter.

56. You contact too many recruiters, especially at the same firm.

57. You don't let your recruiter know when you are working with another recruiter. This can lead to commission conflicts at the same company.

58. You apply for the same positions you are being submitted to as a candidate, and may be disqualified because the company does not want to risk having a recruiter claim a commission if you are

hired directly.

59. You think and act as if recruiters work for you.

60. You don't use recruiters who specialize in your field.

61. You're not honest about your red flag issues, and try to pretend you're perfect.

62. You ask recruiters for meetings out of the blue without saying why the recruiter would want to meet you.

63. You don't debrief the recruiter after an interview.

64. You follow up with the hiring company, and not your recruiter and this makes both you and your recruiter look unprofessional.

65. You decide you will embellish who you are to the recruiter, what you have done, and what you are looking for in a job and salary, and when you interview with the recruiter's client, THEN you will be honest with only the client.

"   **"**

THE INTERVIEW GAME

"Management: A class of semi-skilled corporate hirelings whose rise within the organization correlates directly with the amount of work they delegate to their more-talented underlings."

Anonymous

"The remaining work to finish in order to reach your goal increases as the deadline approaches."

Bove's Theorem

"In the interview process only focus on those things you can control. Let the rest go. To do otherwise just creates needless worry. Unless you WANT to worry."

Bill Cole, MS, MA

76 MISTAKES YOU MAKE WITH RESUMES, CV'S AND COVER LETTERS

Not everyone likes to write, but having a good resume or CV is a fact of interviewing life. A catchy cover letter opens the door just enough so your other materials get read. Following our theme of "don't harm yourself", you'll read these mistakes and possibly see some you can avoid. Or you'll have a good laugh.

1.   Your resume contains no mailing address, no phone number, and no email.

2.   You include religious or political activities, or personal activities on a resume.

3.   You use a personal email address that is non-professional or inappropriate.

4.   You have a file name with an old date, a job title that does not match, or a nickname or an abbreviation that makes no sense, or that is not professional.

5. The cover letter is addressed to the wrong person.

6. Your cover letter is addressed as "Dear Sirs", rather than Dear Hiring Manager, To Whom It May Concern, or better, to the appropriate person.

7. You fail to use complete, grammatically correct sentences, and instead use text message style phrases.

8. You use fancy, colored, bordered or frilly paper, or odd fonts (example-CamelCase) and colors for your resume or cover letter.

9. You are applying for a higher-level tech position but you place on your resume mundane and elementary tasks that any entry-level IT professional knows.

10. As part of your resume package you include endorsement letters from your spouse and children.

11. You scan and PDF dozens of awards, diplomas, transcripts, certificates and citations you have received over the years and send them in as part of your resume package.

12. You attach scratch n' sniff stickers to your resume.

13. You assume the interviewer is male and address the cover letter or voicemail to them with that orientation.

14. On your resume you list current and past job descriptions in either all present tense or all past tense.

15. When you are asked to apply online through the company website you instead ask if you can fax it, email it or mail it.

16. You format your resume using a chronological history of events dating back to high school (especially when you have been out of high school for three or more years).

17. When completing a written application, you write, "see resume" for many of the questions.

18. You fail to mention in the cover letter what job you are applying for.

19. You apply for several positions at the same company at the same time.

20. You provide references of people you have not notified or asked, or of people who may be hostile to you.

21. In mailing or emailing your resume and application materials, you send "bits and pieces" over time, instead of sending the entire piece at once.

22. Your resume says "References available upon request", instead of actually including them.

23. You include your age, religion, marital status, citizenship, race, or hobbies.

24. You provide an exact number of years of professional experience in your opening summary.

25. You list professional experiences more than 15 years old.

26. You attempt to explain why you were fired from previous positions.

27. You list positions and duties, but leave off any accomplishments.

28. You list every job you've ever had.

29. You go into detail on jobs you've had that are not relevant to the field you are in now.

30. You list your salary history and references.

31. Your resume contains photos or artwork.

32. Your resume comes across as sneaky, since you left off any dates.

33. Your resume contradicts your LinkedIn profile.

34. You call your resume a CV and vice versa.

35. You send the interviewer a CV instead of a resume, or vice versa.

36. You don't know how to convert your resume from a list of activities & tasks, and turn them into accomplishments.

37. You begin your cover letter with, "My name is _____."

38. You copy word for word from your resume and paste portions of that onto your cover letter.

39. Your cover letter is more than one page. In fact, it's many pages.

40. Your cover letter goes into your personal life, and your recent struggles, in an effort to generate sympathy.

41. Your cover letter brags that you are perfect for the position, or that the interviewer "will not regret meeting you".

42. Your cover letter gushes about how much you LOVE the company, and that you'd do anything to work there.

43. Your cover letter mainly talks about what you want to get out of the job, not what you can do for the company.

44. Your cover letter starts with weak, boring material, and you save your best content for the end.

45.   Your cover letter fails to mention what makes you unique.

46.   Your cover letter uses weak phrases such as "I think", "I feel" and "I believe", instead of "I know", "I am convinced", and "My bosses tell me I am...".

47.   Your cover letter is not addressed to the exact person it should, and instead it says Dear Sir, or Dear Ms, etc.

48.   Your cover letter has only a temporary location and contact phone and email where you can be reached.

49.   Your cover letter has a stain, is wrinkled, is torn, or has other immediately obvious flaws, begging for rejection.

50.   Your cover letter uses a similar style as that of people typing text messages on their cell phone.

51.   Your cover letter contains contact information that is unprofessional, such as funny or odd email combinations.

52. Your cover letter apologizes for the skills or experience you don't have yet.

53. Your cover letter does not tell a story of you are and you came to where you are now.

54. Your cover letter does not use metrics to calibrate with precision exactly what you have accomplished.

55. Your cover letter includes the phrase "References available upon request", instead of using that space to sell yourself.

56. Your cover letter lacks key words that help employers find targeted applicants.

57. Instead of using a PDF, you copy and paste your resume or cover letter into an email. It arrives to the interviewer with ruined formatting.

58. You have typos and bad grammar and hard to follow ideas in your cover letter.

59. You explain things in your cover letter that are far better done in person.

60. You copy a generic cover letter from the Internet and paste in your own key words.

61. You bring up red flags on your cover letter that immediately scare and turn off the interviewer.

62. You bring up issues in your cover letter that you cannot adequately explain unless you do so in person.

63. You have a negative tone, such as "You probably read many cover letters, and I'm sorry to bother you with one more, but..."

64. You confuse training and education you have with the experience the job is seeking.

65. You see the company has softball leagues and bowling leagues and you say you could really contribute strongly to those teams.

66. Your cover letter clearly shows you don't understand what the company does, or what they're all about.

67. Your cover letter does not match the tone or feel of the company. It does not use the buzzwords they use.

68. Your resume or CV does not go into specifics on jobs you've had. It reads very generally.

69. Your resume or CV has the one-size-fits-all feel, where the interviewer can't really figure out who it's aimed at.

70. Your resume or CV highlights duties instead of actual accomplishments.

71. If you use an objective at the top on your resume or CV, it is generic and doesn't pinpoint what you want.

72. Your resume or CV uses a mix of past tense and present tense wording, even on previous jobs and activities.

73. Your resume or CV uses few action verbs.

74. Your resume or CV has basic errors such as spelling and grammar, that it is easily flagged for immediate rejection.

75. Your resume or CV discloses confi-
    dential information.

76. Your resume or CV has no unifying
    graphical theme, and instead is a
    hodge-podge of various fonts, colors
    and point sizes.

"   "

THE INTERVIEW GAME

"The only way to do great work is to love what you do. If you haven't found it yet, keep looking. Don't settle."

Steve Jobs

"The biggest mistake that you can make is to believe that you are working for somebody else. The driving force of a career must come from the individual. Remember: Jobs are owned by the company. You own your career!"

Earl Nightingale, Motivational Speaker

"Turn a job interview into a conversation, and you will come across more as a potential colleague."

Bill Cole, MS, MA

50 MISTAKES YOU MAKE WHEN YOU INTERVIEW BY TELEPHONE OR VIDEO CONFERENCE

Ahhh. The beloved phone screen. The coveted video interview. We all can't wait to do them. These are mine-fields of potential errors-in-waiting. But there is a way to tip-toe through these potentially destructive zones of worry. That's right. Avoid the mistakes that others make. You'll be different. You'll be smarter.

1. You conduct an interview by video-conference with an inappropriate background scene.

2. You have background noise, people, animals, music or voices that can interrupt the interview.

3. You tell the telephone interviewer that you missed their call because you had another phone interview prior to theirs and you needed to take a break from the interviewing process.

4.   Your computer camera angle is too low or too high.

5.   You don't test the Facetime, Webex, Skype, or other video program you will be using in advance.

6.   You don't test the light sources in advance.

7.   You take another telephone call and place the interviewer on hold.

8.   You use a cell phone instead of a landline and the quality is poor.

9.   You are obviously heard to be walking or in a car as you give the interview.

10. You are driving through a low reception area as you give the interview on your cell phone.

11. You take a phone interview from a company on the fly and forget who they are, since you have been applying to multiple companies, and you call them by the wrong name.

12. You do a telephone interview in less than desirable circumstances, such as

in public, in a noisy environment, or while driving.

13. You do a cell phone interview and forget to turn off all your notifications, such as faxes, alerts, emails, texts, etc.

14. You ask if you can record the conversation.

15. You apologize, saying this is the first time you've ever used this type of technology, and you don't know how to use it.

16. You dress very casually with your hair askew, thinking it will be a phone screen, and at the last minute they ask if you can do a video call.

17. The Skype video icon or photo you use is inappropriate for business.

18. Your video conference screen name is unprofessional.

19. Another call comes in and you put the interviewer on hold to take it.

20. You don't recognize the phone number, answer it unprofessionally, and it turns

out to be the actual interviewer, calling early.

21.   Your phone voicemail greeting is unprofessional.

22.   The interviewer can hear you shuffling papers or making noises.

23.   Even though on the phone feedback is scarce, and rapport is hard to achieve, you ignore trying to achieve rapport.

24.   You don't smile because you figure they can't see you.

25.   You don't answer the phone yourself, and instead you let anyone in the house pick up the phone.

26.   At the last minute the interviewer asks to change to a video connection, instead of a phone interview, and you are not dressed properly.

27.   You expect to land the job, or get an offer over the phone.

28.   You take the phone interview less seriously than an in-person interview.

29. You answer the phone even though you're not ready to begin.

30. You get so comfortable that you lie down and really relax.

31. You don't have a personal branding website to direct the interviewer to view.

32. When using a laptop, you lean on the desk because it's more comfortable.

33. When using a laptop, you put your chin in your hand because it's comfortable.

34. When using a laptop, you slouch down to see the screen better.

35. You tell the interviewer to wait because you have an incoming fax on the same line.

36. You look at the computer screen, not the actual camera.

37. When using a laptop, you run out of battery power.

38. You interview by video, and all goes well until you stand up at the end and the interviewer sees your pajama bottoms.

39. You tell the interviewer that you never have used Skype or some other video conference system and you don't know what you're doing.

40. The interviewer can tell that you are checking email or typing during the video conference meeting.

41. The interviewer can tell that you are web surfing as the meeting progresses.

42. On a phone call you use the speaker function and the interviewer can't hear you very well.

43. You have inadequate technical equipment for video conferencing such as poor bandwidth and Internet connection, a low quality camera or microphone.

44. During a video conference call, the screen freezes and you believe the audio has also frozen, and you mutter some unprofessional things, or swear or yell, yet the interviewer can actually

hear everything.

45. You use your cell phone for a video conference, and hold it in your hand instead of propping it up on the desk.

46. You do a video conference call from your car.

47. You begin a video conference call, and it soon becomes obvious to the interviewer that you are reclining on your bed.

48. It's obvious you are reading your answers from your computer screen.

49. You don't make use of the "picture-in-picture" of yourself on the screen, so you'll be able to see what the other person sees.

50. You wear a shirt with patterns and stripes, causing a distraction in the video transmission.

" **"**

THE INTERVIEW GAME

"You just have to keep trying to do good work, and hope that it leads to more good work. I want to look back on my career and be proud of the work, and be proud that I tried everything.
Yes, I want to look back and know that I was terrible at a variety of things."

Jon Stewart

"Constantly talking isn't necessarily communicating."

Joel Barrish, played by Jim Carrey, in the movie Eternal Sunshine of the Spotless Mind

"You can never truly control your fate, only your reaction to it."

Bill Cole, MS, MA

75 MISTAKES YOU MAKE IN NEGOTIATING A JOB OFFER

Do you know anyone who loves to talk about money? How about negotiating? Do they love that? And don't forget contracts. They're downright exhilarating. Well, if you are going after a new job, those things HAVE to come up sometime. And this chapter gives you just the right amount of smarts on the subject. No, this won't be like law school.

1.   As soon as the interview begins you say, "Let's cut to the chase. How much does this job pay?"

2.   As soon as the interview begins you say, "Tell me what this job pays, because if it's too low, I can save us a lot of time, and leave now".

3.   You tell the interviewer you heard this job pays kind of low, but you are hoping things have changed.

4.   You tell the interviewer you are irritated that the job description did not include salary or package details.

5.   You ask the interviewer if you can get a loan advance before the first paycheck.

6.   You tell a headhunter or internal recruiter too low a target salary, and later regret it after you do your homework.

7.   You dutifully complete all salary history questions for on-line applications.

8.   You tell the interviewer you already have a job offer from another company, and that his offer "Better be good".

9.   You tell the interviewer you already have a job offer from another company, and you arrogantly ask him if he can beat that offer.

10.   You tell the interviewer you already have a job offer from another company, and that you are here today interviewing "just in case that one falls through".

11.   You tell the interviewer you already have a job offer from another company, but it's not so great, and you're curious as to what they have to offer.

12. The interviewer asks what your salary was at your previous job, and you say, "I'm not sure you can afford me".

13. The interviewer asks what your salary was at your previous job, and you pull out a citation from Glassdoor.com showing what you believe you're worth.

14. The interviewer asks what your salary was at your previous job, and you say, "You go first. I'm not going to fall for that old negotiating trick".

15. When you're asked to share information about your previous salary, you inflate your salary and package. Later, when you need to sign the contract, you see a clause that says lying on the application is grounds for dismissal, and they say they may conduct due diligence by contacting your previous employer.

16. The interviewer asks about salary, and you say, "I'm really uncomfortable talking about money".

17. The interviewer asks what your salary was at your previous job, and you say, "None of your business".

18. The interviewer asks what your salary was at your previous job, and you say, "I was afraid you'd ask that".

19. The interviewer asks what your salary was at your previous job, and you say, "I'll tell you that if you tell me your salary now".

20. You ask about salary and benefits in the first interview, or early in the interview process.

21. You say, "I hope these long series of interviews are worth it, once I hear the salary and package you're offering".

22. When asked what salary you are seeking, you give a number right away, instead of making them go first.

23. When asked what salary you are seeking, you say, "It better be higher than what I'm making now, or I've really wasted my time here".

24. When asked what salary you are seeking, you say, "I'm a top performer, and I expect to be paid at the top of your salary scale".

25. When asked what salary you are seeking, you tell the interviewer what you need, regardless of what value you bring to the position.

26. When asked what salary you are seeking, you say, I hope it's $xx. I really want a new boat!!"

27. When asked what salary you are seeking, you give a salary range, hoping to get the top of the range. Then when the manager makes an offer at the bottom of that range, you realize you can't possibly accept it.

28. When asked about your current salary, you inflate it dramatically, and the interviewer knows that can't be true, since they did their own research on your position and industry.

29. The interviewer tells you the salary they are offering and you take it as a personal rejection of your worth.

30. The interviewer tells you the salary they are offering and you say, "That's an insult! I'm worth far more than that!"

31. The interviewer tells you the salary they are offering and you smile slightly, sit taller in your chair, yet say, "That's too low". The interviewer knows you don't play poker well.

32. The interviewer tells you the salary they are offering and you simply say, "That's not what I was looking for", yet you don't have a counter offer.

33. The interviewer tells you the salary they are offering and you make a face, sigh, or exhibit some other emotional reaction to show you are very unhappy with the offer.

34. The interviewer tells you the salary they are offering and you ask if that is the best they can do. Of course they say yes, that's the offer.

35. You focus only on salary and don't add in the value of benefits and perks to the total package.

36. Because you have not strongly established how valuable you will be to the company, you are not in a good position to negotiate a higher salary or package.

37. During the negotiation phase you exhibit a much different personality that you did prior, giving the manager doubts.

38. You plan on making an extensive series of counter-offers by email or phone and the company expects only one or two.

39. You ask so many questions about tiny, picky items on the contract before you sign it that HR or the manager comes to realize you are a high-maintenance person, and they begin to doubt their decision to hire you.

40. You haggle and push and prod about salary like a used car salesman.

41. You're in the HR office or the manager's office with the contract you're about to sign and you ask for last minute concessions from them, because you figure you have them over a barrel now.

42. You think that since you have a "firm verbal offer" or one even in writing in email, that nothing can go wrong. You don't realize that an offer can be withdrawn at any time before you sign it.

43. You make wishy-washy statements as a response to their offer without countering precisely. You say things like, "That's sort of low.", "I think I deserve more", or "Maybe there's room to negotiate", hoping they will increase the offer, without you providing any specific numbers.

44. You say that X is your final number, and if you don't get that, you'll "walk".

45. The company says they don't want to put the offer in writing yet, and you say "No problem".

46. You have a very small list of perks and benefits to negotiate with, relative to your salary.

47. You say you want the job before you even hear the salary and package.

48. In the manager's office, when you begin to discuss salary and package items, you don't write down what is said, and just rely on your memory, or what THEY write down.

49. You come home after the interview and don't send a memorandum of understanding (MOU) or even a friendly

email recapping what was discussed about salary and benefits.

50. You don't know your walk away bottom line with regards to salary and package.

51. You appear so needy and eager to get the job that the interviewer can easily take advantage of you.

52. You assume that certain things are non-negotiable.

53. You bluff and pretend you have job offers from competitors of the company and when the manager asks about these offers they can tell you're bluffing because they know their competitors and what they have been offering.

54. You suddenly are more excited about the salary and package than you were for the rest of the interview about the actual job.

55. The manager agrees to give you future concessions such as a raise or additional perks, but you don't get them in writing.

56. When asked what salary you are seeking, you aggressively play one company against another, asking them to beat another company's offers.

57. When asked what salary you are seeking, you say, "You're the one offering the job. What is it?".

58. You accept the salary and package offered without any negotiation, because you trust people.

59. You accept the salary and package offered without any negotiation, because negotiating makes you uncomfortable.

60. You accept the salary and package offered without any negotiation, because you think this will be the only offer you get.

61. You accept the salary and package offered without any negotiation, because you don't want to upset them, and possibly have them back out.

62. You accept the salary and package offered without any negotiation, because you would feel lots of pressure to perform to their higher expectations

if it went much higher.

63. You reject the salary and package offer out of hand, before you've had time to think about it.

64. You focus too much on salary and overlook the benefits of stock options or other perks.

65. You focus too much on immediate salary and overlook the benefits of growth in the role, advancement, and long-term financial growth in the company.

66. You have not checked around on what the job pays, so you have no way to determine if the salary is competitive or not.

67. You negotiate the contract so hard and so long that the hiring manager has second thoughts about how difficult you will be to work with.

68. When you counter-offer, you ask for lots more In salary, benefits and every perk you can think of.

69. You think that a verbal offer is as binding as a written offer.

70. You negotiate by email rather than phone or in person, and run the risk of having email being misinterpreted in terms of tone and meaning.

71. You negotiate at a time of day when you are not at your sharpest mentally.

72. You know the company has money and you are insulted when the offer is lower than you expect.

73. You exhibit an air of entitlement of how much you're worth to the hiring manager.

74. Once you've gone back and forth and the offer is finalized, the manager sends you the final contract by email and says, "Please sign and return this right away. It's the same details we covered in previous emails". You agree and sign and return it at once without reading it very carefully. Of course it has been re-written in their favor.

75. The contract is quite complex and lengthy, yet instead of having your attorney review it, you read it over

yourself and simply sign and return it for sake of expediency.

"　　　　　**"**

THE INTERVIEW GAME

"Unemployment is no longer just
for philosophy majors."

Anonymous

"Automation has opened up a whole
new field of unemployment."

Anonymous

"When you interview, you are performing. It is
a performance that you must prepare for as
diligently for as if you were speaking in
front of a thousand people. Most people
still get stage fright in front of one
person in an interview."

Bill Cole, MS, MA

49 MISTAKES YOU MAKE ON SITE, BEFORE THE INTERVIEW

Most people just show up to the interview and go for it. I'm a little different. I actually break an interview down into time segments. So here we are, just before you actually begin the interview. What do you do? How do you act? What should you avoid? It's all right here. People think the time before the interview gets underway doesn't count. The interviewer might even tell you that. It could be a trick to let your guard down so they can see how you really operate. But hold on. Interviewers are ALL people of the highest integrity, the best character. They...hold on. Never mind.

1. You ask for adjustments and exceptions to their standard interview process.

2. You don't know how to act and what to say, and what not to say on the "campus tour" or "facility tour" phase of the interview day.

3. You arrive very, very early for the interview and hang around.

4. When asked for when you can interview, you say you need to check with your Mom. You also ask if she or another person can attend the interview.

5. You bring another person to the interview who was not invited.

6. When they change the interview format at the last minute, you object, or visibly act put out.

7. You bring food and drink into the interview.

8. You ask if you can remove your suit coat or sweater because you are hot.

9. You leave your Bluetooth device in your ear.

10. You leave on your hat, sunglasses, overcoat or scarf during an indoor interview.

11. The interviewer kept you waiting and you are observably miffed and say something about it.

12. You are overheard making a phone call while in the lobby, and it is loud, contentious, too personal or compromising.

13. You park your car where it can be observed, and it is less than presentable, inside or out.

14. You walk a great distance to get to the interview, and are out of breath, tired, unkempt and sweaty.

15. You let your guard down with a tour guide, lobby person, driver, guide, handler, assistant, or anyone else who you believe "is not interviewing you". You confide in them, act badly with them or act unprofessionally.

16. The company gives you inaccurate directions to the interview location causing you to arrive late. You proceed to berate the lobby attendant or interviewer and be observably miffed that they caused you trouble.

17. While waiting in the lobby for the interview you close your eyes to rest and the lobby staff reports that you are sleeping.

18. While waiting in the lobby for the interview you strike up a conversation with someone and disclose some things that reflect badly on you, that can be overheard by the lobby staff.

19. You allow the volume of your cell phone to be too high when playing a game or music on it in the lobby.

20. You are running late to the interview and decide not to call to warn them you will be late.

21. The interviewer keeps you waiting just a little bit, and instead of doing the interview, you ask to be rescheduled.

22. You are observed hanging around the lobby or front parking lot either very early before you interview, or the day before.

23. You pull into the company parking lot and engage in behavior that could be construed as undesirable.

24. You arrive quite early to the interview and while waiting, you walk around the premises, looking into offices and down hallways, and generally acting very curious and nosy.

25. You cancel an interview, citing an emergency, only to disclose at the rescheduled interview that the reason you canceled was to go to a less-than-critical social gathering.

26. After making an interview appointment, you call, email or text the interviewer many times to confirm it to "make sure they know" how much passion you have for the position.

27. You cancel the interview at the last minute, without a good reason.

28. You make many requests to change the day or time of the interview.

29. You ask for so many exceptions to their interview procedures, that they realize you are very high-maintenance.

30. You are seen going into the bathroom multiple times, and the lobby personnel assume you are very nervous.

31. You are overheard in the lobby disclosing to a seatmate that you are really just using today's interview for practice.

32.   You tell the administrative assistant what type of coffee you want before being asked if you would like refreshments.

33.   You arrive at the interview wearing very nice branded logo gear, but it's of this company's competitor.

34.   You assume from the name of the interviewer that it is a male and ask to see Mr. so and so in the lobby. (And it is not a man).

35.   While you wait in the lobby, you are so nervous that you continually pace back and forth, or engage in other behaviors that show how keyed up you are.

36.   You eat a lot of the candy or other food offered in the lobby.

37.   You are offered food in the lobby, and ask if you can make a full meal of it.

38.   You make an interview appointment at a very large organization. When you show up, you have forgotten the name of the person you spoke to when you scheduled the interview, or the name of the manager who is interviewing for the position, or what the job is, and you are

not sure what department the job is in.

39. You don't know what to say and how to act when you enter the lobby before the interview.

40. You don't plan well for traveling to the interview, and either get lost, get sidetracked or have a mishap on the way.

41. You don't know how to act with lobby staff once you enter that area.

42. You walk in to the lobby and ask if so and so is there, instead of announcing who you are and why you are there.

43. You make a commotion in the lobby and draw attention to yourself.

44. You arrive in the lobby and ask if you can get some of the free food you've heard the company has for employees.

45. You sit in the lobby and forget to remove your coat and hat.

46. You close your eyes in the lobby to meditate for just a few minutes.

47.   You view a funny video on your phone and laugh out loud in the lobby.

48.   You show up at the correct street address early or on time, but you either don't have the building number or can't find it easily, so you panic and arrive late.

49.   You don't know have a "psych up system" you can use before an interview so you can be calm, yet energized, and remove any mental distractions, self-doubt or negativity.

"   "

THE INTERVIEW GAME

"Think not of yourself as the architect of your career but as the sculptor. Expect to have to do a lot of hard hammering and chiseling and scraping and polishing."

BC Forbes

"I've arrived at the place if I'm not taking a career risk, I'm not happy. If I'm scared, then I know I'm being challenged."

Jim Carrey

"If you align your true self and values with a deep passion for your work, you are not really on a job. You are creating, innovating, playing and leaving a legacy of a body of work that leaves you fully satisfied."

Bill Cole, MS, MA

34 MISTAKES YOU MAKE AS THE INTERVIEW BEGINS

Now you are quite nervous, wondering if there is any way you can escape before this thing gets going. But instead you decide to go for it. That's showing courage. There are plenty of mistakes to be made at this juncture. In fact, due to nerves, people mess up the most here of almost any phase of the interview. They don't achieve rapport. They don't make a good first impression. And they don't get any momentum going. Why? Mistakes. But that's why you'll be reading these mistakes, so you can avoid them and be a great interviewee.

1. You enter the interview room and notice there is an additional person in the room, after you had been told that it was to be a one on one interview. You object and ask what is going on, ask that they be removed, or refuse to continue.

2. You comment or complain that you were kept waiting.

3. When you arrive late to the interview, instead of apologizing and getting on with the interview, you chat on about not only how you had planned to arrive

early, but also how you had printed a map, walked in the wrong direction, and other ways you became late.

4.   You hijack control of the interview, particularly at the beginning, by asking too many questions.

5.   When the interviewer greets you by asking, "How are you today?" You answer "Fine", "Good", "OK", or the like, and don't reciprocate by asking how they are.

6.   You ask the interviewer how long "this will take", as you have somewhere to be later.

7.   Your opening line to the interviewer is "Where is your restroom?"

8.   At the outset of the interview you ask, "Mind if I record this?", as you pull out your recording device.

9.   You tell the interviewer "Your place is hard to find", or "You need better signs out in front", or "your website needs improvement", or "I found a mistake in your literature".

10. You introduce yourself with only your first name.

11. When the interviewer says, "Tell me about yourself", you begin by saying, "My name is ....".

12. You arrive late for the interview and blame someone for giving you bad directions.

13. After walking in to the panel interview room, and being directed to sit in a particular chair, you decline and instead opt to sit in a chair you prefer.

14. You take a seat before your interviewer does.

15. You place your briefcase, notepad, purse or device on the table without asking.

16. You carry multiple bags and items you must juggle as you stand up, greet the interviewer and walk.

17. While you are waiting alone in the conference room, you act inappropriately, by talking to yourself, poking around, exercising, napping or anything

else.

18.   When offered water or some other beverage by the interviewer, you turn it down.

19.   When offered coffee by the interviewer, you turn it down and criticize the drink as being "unhealthy".

20.   You sit down before being directed to do so.

21.   You continue to wear your sunglasses on top of your head, or behind your neck, once indoors.

22.   You forget to remove your heavy winter coat once indoors.

23.   As you reach out to shake the hand of the interviewer you realize your hand is sweaty, yet you shake their hand anyhow.

24.   You walk into the interview room as you are eating.

25.   You sit down and remove your shoes to be more comfortable.

26. The interviewer might switch the interview format at the last minute from 1-1 to panel, or some other format, and you object.

27. You don't know how to start off on the "right foot" so you connect with the interviewer and make a great first impression.

28. You don't know how to make a great first impression.

29. You don't know how to behave before the interview starts—and after, in the hallways and lobby, when the "official interview" is not taking place.

30. You walk in the interview room and instead of shaking hands with the interviewer(s), you wave.

31. You walk in the interviewer's office as you are talking on your cell phone.

32. You arrive late with a cup of coffee in your hand, demonstrating that coffee is more important to you than the job.

33. You arrive to the interview early and ask if you can begin early.

34. You walk in and drop or toss your backpack on the table or floor with a thud.

"   **"**

THE INTERVIEW GAME

"Please don't misconstrue my 14 jobs as 'job-hopping.' I have never quit a job."

Anonymous

"My career is just kind of crazy."

David Spade

"Every advancement you make in your career is new territory. You need to embrace the unknown to move ahead."

Bill Cole, MS, MA

31 MISTAKES YOU MAKE WITH INTERVIEWS INVOLVING FOOD AND DRINK

Many interviews in offices don't involve food and drink, but some do, even if they're just water and crackers. Then you have the "official lunch interview" or even the more dreaded "official dinner interview". These really put people on edge. That's mainly because you don't really know how to behave. But here you can learn about all that. And then you won't get indigestion.

1.   You are taken to a lunch interview and become picky about the type of restaurant, the menu, your order, the wait staff or anything else.

2.   You order alcohol without being invited by the interviewer.

3.   You drink more alcohol or eat more food than appropriate.

4.   You order items that are above and beyond normal prices, or against the

grain of how the interviewer is ordering.

5.   You sit down before everyone else.

6.   You order finger food or food you must pick up.

7.   You make noises as you eat.

8.   You order very unhealthy-looking food.

9.   You pull out a bag of food and announce that you "like to eat healthy".

10. You order a hard to eat, sloppy or unusual meal.

11. You try out a new dish you have never had before.

12. You say you are not hungry and let everyone else eat while you sit there.

13. You order a large meal and ask for a doggie bag.

14. You eat a huge amount of food by going to back to the buffet table

multiple times.

15. You are the only one to order an appetizer and dessert.

16. You display poor manners of any type.

17. You treat the wait staff poorly.

18. You forget to mention the meal in your thank you note.

19. You let your guard down, particularly with someone near your own age, who may be there to test you on that.

20. You immediately begin selling yourself before the social niceties have begun.

21. You are very picky when it comes to ordering (substitutions, asking too many questions, etc.) and how you eat your food.

22. You feel compelled to answer a question, even though you still have food in your mouth.

23. You focus mainly on your food and ignore the people.

24. You eat fast in order to be able to talk more.

25. You complain about your food, and even send it back.

26. You offer to pay the bill, even though it's the host's meeting.

27. You negatively compare this restaurant to your favorite restaurant.

28. You ask the host why they didn't select a different restaurant.

29. You nervously fumble your utensils and are demonstrably upset.

30. You reach across the table.

31. You yell across the table to other people.

"

"

THE INTERVIEW GAME

"I graduated from college and went on one job interview and was laughing in my own head because I wouldn't hire me."

Daniel Tosh

"Recruiting is hard. It's just finding the needles in the haystack. You can't know enough in a one-hour interview. So, in the end, it's ultimately based on your gut. How do I feel about this person? What are they like when they're challenged? I ask everybody that: "Why are you here?" The answers themselves are not what you're looking for. It's the meta-data."

Steve Jobs

"Confidence in interviewing is demystifying the mysterious and knowing the unknowns as much as possible."

Bill Cole, MS, MA

348 VERBAL MISTAKES YOU MAKE DURING THE INTERVIEW

I know what you're thinking. Wow! That's a lot of mistakes, 348! Who can possibly make THAT many mistakes in one interview? I'm not sure I even want to meet that person. People make all sorts of verbal gaffs and put their foot in their mouth all the time in interviews. But that won't be you. That's because you'll be armed with these precision details about the mistakes OTHER people make. And you? Well, you'll be sitting pretty. Making a good impression with the interviewer.

1. You brag about and specifically point out your body art and piercings.

2. You talk about your religious views and even begin to convince the interviewer that they should consider your religion.

3. You dominate and take the interview over by asking too many questions, making too many comments and by generally being controlling.

4.   When asked when you can start, you are less than enthusiastic and cite numerous obstacles to beginning immediately.

5.   You attempt to "make friends" with the interviewer.

6.   You complain about service providers at the restaurant you just visited when you are at the interview.

7.   You ask questions or answer questions in a way that show you have not been listening.

8.   You ask if the interviewer minds if you remove your suit coat or sweater.

9.   You call the interviewer by the wrong name, the wrong title or wrong rank, or you call them by their first name, when it really should be their last name.

10.   You ask the woman interviewer if she prefers Ms., Miss, or Mrs. as a title.

11.   You ask the woman interviewer who appears rather large in the torso area if she is pregnant.

12. You give the interviewer advice, of any sort.

13. You tell jokes or turn various aspects of the interview into something humorous.

14. The interviewer asks you to choose between two less than ideal options and you dutifully choose one, instead of saying both or creating a new option.

15. You say "If I join the team...", which makes it sound doubtful, instead of "When I join the team...".

16. You highlight similarities you have with the interviewer (clubs, teams, schools, associations, people, etc.) in order to make him believe you should get the job based primarily on those associations.

17. You complain about the weather, the public transportation, the hotel or other situations you encountered on the way to the interview.

18. You announce to the interviewer that you are interviewing elsewhere. You also do it in a bragging sort of way to let them know you are "popular and desirable" and that they should want

you more.

19. You call the interviewer or the organization by the wrong name.

20. The interviewer asks you, "What advice would you give your former boss, if he were to ask you?" and you go into detail with all your boss's faults.

21. You tell the interviewer he should hire you because you would be a great addition to the company softball team.

22. You tell the interviewer the company has good benefits, which is good because you are going to need to take a lot of leave in the next year.

23. In multiple ways, you continue to tell the interviewer, "I'm so perfect for you. You should hire me now".

24. You use assumptive phrases to show your passion for the position, such as, "My whole career pathway has been leading up to this job, so let's do this", and "I'm a true star. I'll give your company the advantage of having me first".

25. You tell the interviewer you are a "Jack of all trades" and that you can handle any job they have.

26. You describe your job activities instead of your accomplishments.

27. You get so hung up on trying to remember exact dates and people's names from your resume that the interview grinds to a halt.

28. Because of your fears about an uncertain economy, you ask about severance packages for failures or mergers before the interviewer even gets to the heart of the interview.

29. During the interview you are somehow able to read what the interviewer is writing from across the table, by doing some mental gymnastics of inverting the page upside down. As you mentally transpose this, you realize he wrote something critical of you. You then proceed to argue with him about that.

30. After being told you won't be offered a position, you demand to be reimbursed for parking and travel expenses.

31. You hijack the interview by asking too many questions, or by asking a series of questions at the very outset, as if you are in charge.

32. You talk about jobs you have had many years ago, or about irrelevant jobs, instead of describing experience you've had that is pertinent to the position you are seeking.

33. You make a hard to believe announcement such as "Working at your organization has always been my ultimate dream".

34. You imply or say directly that internships were actually real paying jobs.

35. Most or all of the questions you ask are of the closed type rather than open questions.

36. You tell the interviewer their "search is over", as they have now found their new star employee.

37. When asked about weaknesses or problems, you attempt to spin tough situations into ones with only positive

outcomes.

38.   You admit to being nervous.

39.   You bad-mouth or denigrate anything or anyone at the interviewing organization.

40.   You attempt to one-up or to top the interviewer on various topics or issues.

41.   You don't laugh at the interviewer's attempts at humor.

42.   You make the interviewer wrong by correcting their questions, their company, their grammar, their assumptions, their values, or anything else.

43.   You cut the interviewer off mid-sentence.

44.   You editorialize on the quality of the interviewer's questions.

45.   You attempt to "make friends with the interviewer" and when they do not reciprocate, you are visibly upset.

46.   The interviewer asks you what you believe is the exact same question as before, and you make a face or simply

answer it again.

47. The interviewer asks you a question that you can barely understand, and you decide to fake your way through the answer.

48. You ask if you can "be paid under the table".

49. During an interview, you say, "I don't want to be bored in this position."

50. You say, "I am here to learn your business so then in three years I can go out and run the same business."

51. You disclose that you may not be at your best in the interview because you got drunk last night, or had a hot date that lasted all night.

52. When asked what you don't like in a supervisor, you say, "I hate bosses that ask stupid questions".

53. You mention to the interviewer that "you are also available for consulting work", or say you would be open to working part time if the full time

position did not work out.

54. When the interviewer asks what you are looking for in your career, you tell them "anything where I have a job and that pays well".

55. In an effort to appear chummy or to show what you have in common, you give a greeting in Spanish to a Latino-looking interviewer.

56. After you give what you believe is a particularly good or even great answer, you say to the interviewer, "Was that a good answer?", "That was a good one, right?", "That was my best answer yet, right?", "How does that compare to other answers you have heard?".

57. When you are asked the question "Why do you want to work for our company?" you provide answers that are focused on you instead of how you can benefit the company.

58. You inappropriately make light of things that should not be made fun of.

59. The interviewer spends quite a lot of time talking about themselves and the company, without asking you many

questions. You are obviously miffed and interrupt them to "get the interview back on track".

60. You describe your last job, and it is clear that you are "not over it", and you display emotionality, as if you are in a therapy session.

61. You ask so many questions the inter-viewer thinks he is being interviewed.

62. You ask questions about the inter-viewer's background and credentials that make it seem like you are questioning their credibility.

63. You give answers that are evasive and deflecting.

64. You ask the interviewer "What you are doing well so far", or you ask for praise.

65. You announce that you like "lots of guidance and training" and you actually want someone to mentor you.

66. When asked how you would approach a particular problem example posed to you, you state that you "would call your mother for advice".

67. When asked to describe your weaknesses you state, "I have no weaknesses—only "weaker strengths."

68. You use jargon as if you are already an insider in the interviewer's field.

69. You get in the pattern of constantly asking a question right back after the interviewer asks their question.

70. When the interviewer presses you to reveal confidential information about a present or former employer, you respond with details, showing you can't be trusted.

71. When asked why you want to change jobs, you inappropriately disclose some of the bad habits of your previous or current boss.

72. You use language that does not match the level of position you are seeking. For example, you say you want this "job", not "the position", or "role" or "opportunity".

73. You use slang, non-professional, or casual language, or actually swear or use profanities.

74. The interviewer asks you how quickly it would take you to come up to speed on a certain programming language the company uses and you respond with a rant about why they should change to a better one, or your preferred software.

75. You tell the interviewer that his boss and you are relatives, friends or acquaintances.

76. You ask how you can be promoted, get a raise, get a new role, or how to advance yourself.

77. You tell the interviewer of the restrictions you have about your employment, such as days you cannot work, hours you want off, or things you won't do.

78. You prematurely discuss compensation, time off and benefits.

79. You notice that the interviewer has the same brand purse, bag or other items as you, and you make mention of that.

80. You often quote famous people as part of your answer.

81. You ask the interviewer if they can have coffee with you later, since there is more you have to tell them about your candidacy.

82. You ask the interviewer questions about the company that can easily be found on the company web site.

83. The interviewer initiates small talk about sports and you bash their team while praising yours.

84. The interviewer initiates small talk about music and you praise your musical choices while putting down their preferences.

85. After giving what you consider to be a poor answer, you are visibly upset and you put yourself down, saying something like, "What an idiotic answer!", or "Man, I'll never get a job with answers like that!", or "That was NOT the answer I practiced all week!".

86. You tell the interviewer to call your mother, because she has some good things to say about you, but she couldn't attend In person.

87.   You show the interviewer your jewelry and tell them how proud you are of it and how you acquired it.

88.   You ask the interviewer for personal or career advice, on topics completely unrelated to the position.

89.   The interviewer delves into some small talk with you in order to build rapport with you and you immediately change the subject, dismissing what they said.

90.   When the interviewer asks if you have any career regrets or things that you wished you'd have done differently, you reply with a too-honest statement that opens up a conversation that becomes negative.

91.   When the interviewer asks, "What types of people do you not like?", you give an emotional, lengthy answer that shows you are hard to get along with.

92.   You attempt to ingratiate yourself with the interviewer by enthusiastically agreeing with all their viewpoints.

93.   You ask the interviewer questions about their career or current role that are too probing, personal or off-topic.

94. You disrespect their interview process and procedures by asking for special exceptions or allowances.

95. You say things to try to make the interviewer feel sympathy for you.

96. You say things to try to make the interviewer feel guilty so they hire you.

97. You share intimate personal details, thinking the interviewer will "bond" with you.

98. The interviewer and you are engaged in small talk, discussing the day's media news, including local, national and international happenings, and you offer your strong, inflexible opinions on religion, politics and other sensitive issues.

99. You refuse to answer a question for whatever reason.

100. After less than half of the interview is over, you become impatient and say to the interviewer, "Let's cut to the chase. Do I have the job?"

101. You listen to only the first part of the interviewer's question, assume you know the rest of what they are asking, stop listening, and proceed to give the wrong answer.

102. The interviewer cuts the interview time short, and you are visibly miffed, and complain that you "traveled a long distance to get here".

103. The interviewer comments on how nervous you appear and you deny it.

104. The interviewer uses technical terms and jargon you do not understand yet you don't ask what they mean, and instead attempt to fake it.

105. The interviewer asks questions about items that are on your resume, and you are visibly bothered by this and even say, "This is wasting my time".

106. When asked a question you don't know, you tell the interviewer to wait while you Google it.

107. You ask the interviewer if you can "call your therapist for advice".

108. You ask questions that are confidential, that the interviewer cannot answer.

109. You turn the tables on the interviewer and ask them about their weaknesses and to have them convince you they would be good to work for.

110. The interviewer asks, "What about this job do you think you will like least?", and you go on at length about your concerns.

111. The interviewer asks another question while you are still answering the previous one, and you are observably miffed, and tell them to "stop interrupting me".

112. The interviewer asks you to complete a puzzle or task that has no practical solution and you see it as silly and off-task, and say so.

113. When asked how the position would contribute to your professional goals and plans you reply, "This is a placeholder. My real dream is to save enough money to travel in Europe for six months".

114. In an early interview you ask, "When will I be promoted?", "When can I expect a raise?", or "How much will I be making relative to my co-workers?".

115. You ask how many "warnings" or "write-ups" the company allows before firing someone.

116. You ask what the company considers acceptable in terms of an absenteeism record.

117. You ask if you can limit the amount of travel in the position.

118. You ask if relocation is a necessary part of the position.

119. You ask if you can telecommute.

120. You ask if you can job share, or if the position could be restructured as a part-time position.

121. You question the reasons behind company policies and procedures.

122. You use qualifying words and phrases, such as "hopefully", "perhaps", "kind

of", "for the most part", and "sort of".

123. When asked whom you admire as a role model, you supply the name of an infamous, corrupt, criminal, nefarious individual and attempt to justify your choice.

124. When the interviewer describes what they want a candidate to avoid doing once on the job, you respond defensively by repeatedly stating, "I wouldn't do that", or "That doesn't apply to me".

125. When asked about your experience in a particular area, you answer that you have watched a lot of television on that topic and you therefore feel quite qualified and experienced.

126. In response to a question posed by the interviewer that you don't like, or that you can't answer, you say, "Pass", or "Next question".

127. You tell the interviewer, "I'm sold on this company. You've passed my qualification test."

128. You announce that you love the company and ask, "When would you

like me to start?"

129. You announce that in addition to this potential position, you plan to continue your own part-time business on the side, and that the working times may sometimes conflict.

130. You primarily ask closed questions rather than open questions.

131. You are asked to name some influential people in your industry, and you do, while also trashing one or more of them. Unknown to you, the interviewer was mentored by one of them.

132. When you are asked, "Why do you want to leave company X?" you give far too many negative details.

133. When asked your goals, you give an answer that has nothing to do with your career, the industry or their organization.

134. You begin by asking the interviewer, "What's in this job for me?", or "Sell me on this job", or "Convince me why I should work for you".

135. You are engaged in a series of interviews over the course of a day and when you arrive at the final interview and are asked if you have any questions, you state, "No.", since you used them all up in the previous interviews.

136. You are engaged in a series of interviews over the course of a day and after the first interview, when asked the same or similar questions by the following interviewers, you state, "The other guy asked me that", "I already answered that", or "Not this question again.", or "Will everyone be asking the same questions here?"

137. You ask the interviewer, " Once I'm done with all of my work for the day, can I go home early? "

138. When the interviewer asks, "Do you have any questions for me?", you say, "What's the worst thing about working here?", or some other negative question.

139. The interviewer asks you if you know someone they know from your previous company, and you respond, "Yes, I do, and they are crazy".

140. The main focus of your questions revolve around what you want to get out of the position, and not how you can contribute to the company.

141. You ask how long it takes to qualify for a "company sabbatical".

142. You say "Yeah" or "Yup" or "Uh-huh" rather than "Yes", and "Nope" or "Nah" or "Uh-uh" for "No", or simply nod your head silently.

143. You finish your answers by saying, "So that's it", or "I guess that's all I've got on that".

144. Before answering, you repeat, word for word, the interviewer's question.

145. You use the "Yes, but" formula, saying things like, "Yes, I can do that, but that's not my strength".

146. You use the phrase "Of course". You tack on "of course" at the end of your sentences, as if to say "Of course I do that, you idiot".

147. In describing how you were "laid off or let go" from a previous position, you

use inflammatory language such as "I was fired, canned, had a conflict, was written up, was bounced, good riddance, losers, etc".

148. You begin answering the question "Tell me about yourself" by saying, "My name is John Jones...".

149. You tell politically incorrect jokes, or make attempts at humor at someone else's expense.

150. The interviewer asks you what you consider a "dumb question" and you visibly react, or state that the question is "not valid".

151. The interviewer asks you a question that stumps you, and you say, "I didn't expect that question".

152. The interviewer asks you a question that you don't understand, and you say, "What?", "Can you repeat that?", or "I don't understand".

153. The interviewer asks you why you were fired, or why you have a gap in your resume, and you give a defensive answer that is over-explanatory and

rambling.

154. The interviewer asks you about a weakness, and you give one that is irrelevant to the position.

155. You ask what the company considers to be a "good absenteeism record".

156. You give an answer you don't like, and say "I can't believe I just said that", or "I wish I had thought that through more", or "would you like to know more?", or "Was that OK?"

157. After hearing the interviewer's question you say, "I'll pass on that question", or "Can you ask me a different question?"

158. You ask the interviewer to qualify or specify their scenario or case study question in detail, because you are feeling insecure about answering it as is.

159. You tell them you are the perfect person for this position.

160. You tell them that they will love you if they hire you.

161. You tell them you are far more qualified than any other applicant they'll ever see.

162. You tell them their company has fatal flaws, but you will be able to rescue them from disaster.

163. You tell them you'll do anything they ask if you get the job.

164. You tell the interviewer you need the job very, very badly.

165. You tell the interviewer you don't agree with how their question is worded.

166. After the question is delivered, you tell the interviewer you were dreading them asking you that question.

167. You tell the interviewer you are over-qualified for the position, with a haughty tone, making them think you don't want to be there, and that the position is beneath you.

168. Because you think you know the question the interviewer is asking, you cut him off and finish the question for him.

169. The interviewer asks how you would do a certain procedure using a particular computer program or product they use and you say, "I would never use such an inferior program. I use ABC."

170. You say you are feeling insecure because you did not have enough time for interview practice.

171. When asked the question, "Where do you see yourself in five years?", you give an answer unrelated to the current interview position, or the field or company.

172. You tell them you want to keep your part-time job, "just in case", or because it is your passion.

173. You ask to see the break room, recreational facilities and where you can "take a smoke".

174. The interviewer asks you to "walk me through your resume", and indignantly say, "Why didn't you take the time to read it?", or you are observably miffed.

175. When asked how you get along with people, you state, "My co-workers

didn't like me, but I think it was because they were intimidated by me."

176. When asked, "Tell me about yourself", you mainly give personal likes and dislikes, hobbies and activities and personal issues.

177. In the next interview in a series of interviews that day, you comment that the previous interview went poorly, or that you did not like the interviewer.

178. The interviewer describes things or explains things to you and you continually respond with "I know".

179. The interviewer describes a series of things their company frowns upon to you and you continually respond with "I wouldn't do that", defensively.

180. The interviewer cuts the interview short, and you are observably miffed and make an objection that you "didn't get all your allotted time".

181. The interviewer introduces himself by his first and last name, and you call him by his first name.

182. The interviewer asks, "Do you have experience in XYZ?" and you glibly say "No, but I am a really fast learner, so I am sure I can pick it up quickly."

183. You ask the interviewer, "Are you going to be my boss? You're so much older than I am!". "How come you're interviewing me?" "Am I just going to see you today, or will I see the boss?"

184. You make a mistake in answering and say, "That's my ADHD mind acting up again", or, "I really need to adjust my medication", or "I should think before I speak!"

185. You continually say, "To be honest", or "Honestly" or "Frankly", or "To be candid".

186. When you are asked why you believe you'd be good at this job you say, "My Mom thinks I'm a great fit for this position".

187. When asked to describe a successful achievement of yours, you over exaggerate and claim your company improved its profits by 150%, attributable solely to your efforts.

188. After the interviewer explains the role of the position you say, "Can I be honest? That job sounds really boring! Isn't there something else I can do?"

189. You say to the interviewer, "You must be busy because your office is really messy.", or "I know you're really busy, since we started this interview late".

190. When asked why you want to change jobs, you answer, "For the past year in my current position I've been totally bored, with nothing to do".

191. When asked what you know about the company, you say, "I haven't really had time to look at your website yet".

192. You tell the interviewer that you "would love to have their job".

193. You tell the interviewer, in response to their question, "That question I would rather answer with the owner of the company".

194. When the interviewer asks you a question, you say, "Wouldn't the example I gave about XYZ cover that?".

195. When the interviewer asks you a question, you say, "As I said before...", or "As I was saying...", or "As I stated in my previous answer...", as a lead in to your answer.

196. You tell the interviewer that some of the material you may be telling him is confidential, and you ask if he can be trusted to keep secrets.

197. In response to what you consider a too-basic question, you state, "Isn't that obvious?", or "Will the questions get better?"

198. You ask the interviewer, "What do you dislike about working here?'

199. You ask the interviewer thinly veiled questions like, "Why are there so many open positions?", or "I understand the company stock just went down", indicating you are suspicious about the health of the company.

200. When the interviewer asks what you consider to be an odd question, you ask, "What relevance does this question have to the position I am seeking?"

201. You patronize the interviewer by asking them, as you explain some detailed matter, "Is this too technical for you?"

202. Instead of simply answering "No", and then explaining, you say "No, no, no, no before answering.

203. You become frustrated in explaining something the interviewer is not yet understanding and say, "You just don't understand what I'm saying", or "Let me simplify that for you".

204. You meet the interviewer, who is similar to you in some way (age, gender, race, etc.) and you exclaim, "Oh, I'm so glad I got an interviewer just like me!"

205. You tell the interviewer you really don't want the job, but that you are using the interview as a practice session.

206. You describe your work background with obvious generic statements that serve more as job descriptions than actual accomplishments.

207. You ask for the contact information of the person who you would be replacing so you can "interview them" about the

position.

208. In response to the question, "What is your weakness?", you answer flippantly with a response like "I eat too much rocky road ice cream", in an effort to be cute and humorous.

209. You begin every answer with, "Well", "Sure", "OK", "My answer is...", or "The way I would answer that is...".

210. You tell the interviewer you don't like working with people who have less education than you.

211. After some time, you suddenly announce, "Now it's MY turn to ask the questions!"

212. Upon being asked why you left your last job, you reply, "Everyone there was out to get me".

213. You ramble and give long answers, and fail to recognize or respond to any attempts by the interviewer to hurry you up or to break in so they can ask more questions.

214. You tell the interviewer that you are giving him a B+, and that his grade would have been higher if he had asked better questions.

215. You believe that the interviewer does not like you, or he is not doing a good job, so you ask, "Is there anyone else who can interview me right now?"

216. You ask what "the employee discount is" or what other perks employees get.

217. You ask the interviewer to wait while you make a post on social media.

218. You rest on a past accomplishment, like graduating from a top school, and give this as the main reason to hire you now, with no statement of how that can help the company.

219. After the interviewer asks what you believe to be a question you don't like, you say, "Why do you want to know THAT?

220. You ask the interviewer to take a selfie with you.

221. You ask the interviewer an unending string of qualifying, probing, testing questions designed to determine, "Let me see if this job is a good fit for me, and if I will be happy here", rather than convincing the interviewer how you can help their organization.

222. You give the interviewer a lecture on how the private sector pays better than the public sector and that since the salary the interviewer is offering was the same as your present salary they should offer you the position at a higher rate because "Everybody knows the private sector pays more than the public sector".

223. If you're currently employed, you tell your interviewer that you could start work right away, and that giving any extra notice to your current boss is unnecessary.

224. You are asked about your weakness and you say you need to "really think about that".

225. You interrupt the interviewer as they are speaking.

226. You say "As I said before...", and the interviewer feels put down.

227. You engage in cross-talk where you and the interviewer speak at the same time.

228. You don't wrap up your answers properly, and instead just let them trail off, when you say, "...so yeah...".

229. You name drop and brag about whom you know.

230. You make excuses or apologize for any deficits in your resume.

231. You repeat the interviewer's question word for word as you begin your answer.

232. You say "What? Huh?, "I don't understand", or "That's a confusing question".

233. Your response to a question you don't know, or to one you don't like is, "I'll pass", or "Can you ask me a different question?".

234. Instead of saying yes or no, you say yup, nope, uh-huh and yeah.

235. You tell the interviewer, in response to their question, "I'd rather talk about this instead".

236. Rather than simply answering the question, you add all sorts of editorial comments in advance, such as saying, "That's a good question.", "Thank you for that question", "I'm glad you asked me that question.", "I knew you would ask me that question.", "I was hoping you would ask me that question.", or "I studied for that question."

237. In a series of interviews, when you get the same question with a new interviewer, you say, "They asked me that question in my other interview."

238. You evaluate the degree of difficulty in the questions by saying, "That's a tough question." and "That's an easy one."

239. You say, "That's a question my coach and I worked on."

240. Rather than silently wait for the next question after you answer, you add all sorts of editorial comments such as

"I'm rambling, so I better stop now", "I had one more thing to add, but I can't recall it right now, so I'll stop.", "So I guess I'm done", "So that's it" and "So....yeah".

241. You apologize for the quality of your answers by saying "The answer I rehearsed was better that this", "That came out different than the answer I practiced", "Sorry. I wish I had a better answer", "I know that wasn't very good" and, "I'll do better next question".

242. You say you are very particular about the kind of computer and software you use.

243. You make demands on the kind of office space they say they will give you.

244. When asked "Tell me about yourself" or "What is your background" you launch into a detailed tour of your resume.

245. When asked "Walk me through your resume" you actually begin reading your resume to the interviewer.

246. When asked "Walk me through your resume" you go through every detail

you can think of, and lose the interviewer.

247. Your answer to "Tell me about yourself" contains personal elements that are irrelevant to a business situation.

248. Your answer to "Tell me about yourself" contains no personal elements that are relevant to a professional school situation.

249. Instead of clarifying what the interviewer seeks in a question, you assume and launch into your answer.

250. You say you have not had time to review the job description fully.

251. The interviewer asks what you know about their organization and you say, "I really don't know too much".

252. The interviewer asks what your career goals are and you say you "live one day at a time".

253. The interviewer asks what you know about the position and you say, "I was hoping you could tell me".

254. The interviewer asks if you are excited about the position, and you merely answer, "Yes", instead of elaborating and showing your enthusiasm.

255. You say you'll "try to do your best" if you get the job, instead of saying you'll give the job 100% of your energy, focus and dedication every day.

256. You give a fantastic answer, but then the interviewer says, "That's not what I asked".

257. You ask if the company will be checking your references.

258. You ask if you can work from home, or if you can do so a certain percentage of time.

259. You ask about employee discounts.

260. You ask the interviewer if you can meet for coffee later, because you have "so much to tell them about you".

261. You tell the interviewer you are cold or hot and to please change the air conditioning or heating.

262. You ask if there are any other jobs open at the company.

263. You ask if you can leave early if you finish your work.

264. You tell the interviewer about a great job you just missed getting at another company.

265. You ask questions about pay and benefits in early interviews that should be reserved for later interviews.

266. You ask so many vetting questions about the company the interviewer feels they are being interrogated.

267. When asked to describe your weakness, you give one that is a deal-killer.

268. When asked to describe your weakness, you give one that sounds implausible.

269. When asked to describe your weakness, you give one that would make you hard to work with.

270. When asked, "Why do you want to work here", you say "Your office is a short

commute for me".

271. When asked, "Why do you want to work here", you say "This would be a great stepping-stone in my career".

272. When asked, "Why do you want to work here", you say "I really need a job".

273. When asked, "Why do you want to work here", you say "My significant other put their foot down and said it's now or never".

274. When asked, "Why do you want to work here", you say "Your company is as good as any".

275. When asked, "Why do you want to work here", you say "I really don't want to work now, but I need something in the off-season from my main gig".

276. When asked, "Why do you want to work here", you say "I want to get an MBA and I heard you have tuition reimbursement".

277. When asked, "Why do you want to work here", you say, "Your company name

will look great on my resume".

278. When asked, "Why do you want to work here", you say "I hear you have free food and stuff".

279. When asked why you left your last job you say that no one appreciated your brilliance.

280. When asked why you left your last job you say you had a boss who had it in for you.

281. When asked why you left your last job you say you were treated unfairly.

282. When asked why you left your last job you say, "Why do you need to know that?"

283. When asked why you left your last job you say, "It was just a job. Who really cares?"

284. When asked why you left your last job you say you really don't want to talk about it.

285. When asked why you left your last job you unload all your emotional baggage

about that job on the interviewer.

286. When asked why you left your last job you say you don't really know.

287. When asked why you left your last job you say you had unfair job performance reviews.

288. When asked why you left your last job you say you never should have taken that job in the first place.

289. You use profanity.

290. When asked a very basic or simple question, you react as if it is beneath you to even consider it.

291. When asked a very basic or simple question, you ask how that is relevant to the position.

292. You ask how much of the job will be boring, and beneath your actual capability level.

293. When asked about a concern the interviewer has, you over-explain, causing them to become suspicious.

294. When asked about something in your resume that happened a while back, you say, "That was so long ago I have no idea", rather than saying you'll get that data for the interviewer.

295. You tell the interviewer how you are the perfect person for the job, and how no one else could even come close to you capabilities.

296. Before the interviewer can ask the first question, you take charge and begin selling yourself in a dramatic way.

297. You ask if there is a dress code, adding that you like to dress in comfort while you work.

298. You use the interview as your personal therapy session, and share far too much with the interviewer.

299. You give a very long-winded answer to a question that could have been answered in less than a few seconds.

300. You give a very short answer to a question that really required a much longer response.

301. You rarely tell stories or give examples.

302. When asked if you are interviewing elsewhere, you say no, and the interviewer does not see you as being "in the hunt", or popular.

303. When asked if you are interviewing elsewhere, you say yes, and go on to over-explain all about the other companies, leaving the interviewer with the feeling that they are not your top choice.

304. When asked if you are interviewing elsewhere, you tell them the companies, which are either far above or far below their company, and they get the idea that you are a bad fit for them.

305. When asked if you have references, you say not now, and that you'd need to get some.

306. When asked if you have references, you say maybe, and that you need to confirm that the people will agree to vouch for you.

307. The interviewer asks you to conduct the interview in a non-traditional location,

such as outside, when walking, in a car, in a hallway, and you feel and act miffed.

308. The interviewer brings up an additional aspect of the job not listed in the position announcement, and you object, saying you were misled.

309. You refer to yourself as an extreme introvert, and shy.

310. You seem to have an excuse for everything you don't know, can't explain or don't do well.

311. You have an air of blaming other people for your shortcomings.

312. You make light of a serious matter the interviewer brings up.

313. You tell the interviewer you don't want to be assigned any boss that is a "micromanager".

314. You ask concerned questions about overtime, indicating that you really don't like it.

315. You ask if you can get a lot of overtime.

316. In an early interview, you ask about a paternity or maternity leave policy, indicating you might be away for some time.

317. You ask how often people get raises.

318. You ask if anyone will be checking out your social media activities.

319. You have similar experience the company is seeking, but you frame it as irrelevant.

320. Instead of saying yes or no, you nod your head or shrug your shoulders.

321. You don't segue into additional material the interviewer should know, and instead simply obediently answer what is put to you.

322. You pretend to be someone you are not, and the interviewer can see through that.

323. You think interviewers will be intimidated by your lofty accomplishments, so you downplay them.

324. You refer to the company by the wrong name, or use a slang term for it that is not well-received.

325. You utilize cliche phrases such as "I'm a people person and team player", without adding any details.

326. You describe yourself as a generalist or a specialist when the position is just the opposite.

327. You react emotionally when you learn the job does not pay what you expected.

328. You heard some sales advice called ABC that says you should "Always Be Closing", so you continuously ask the interviewer if you are a good fit, if they like you, and if you are the best candidate.

329. You have stellar accomplishments, but you come across as far too humble or minimizing about them, making the interviewer suspicious.

330. You ask the interviewer to repeat the question because you were distracted by your cell phone notification vibrating

in your pocket.

331. When asked if you would bend or break the rules in order to expedite a project, you say, "Whatever it takes. Rules were made to be broken".

332. You ask the interviewer if they've "checked you out on social media yet".

333. You use the word "I" when describing team projects.

334. You refer to people who make mistakes as losers, bozos and jerks.

335. When asked what your goals are for the next five years, you state what you want past this job, but never mention how excited you are and what you will do in the role you are applying for now.

336. You ask, "How am I doing? Are you going to hire me?"

337. You use crude, street language, or paint dark and unhappy pictures with your answers.

338. After many of the interviewer's questions, you say, "Why do you ask?",

or "Why do you need to know that?"

339. When asked to describe yourself, you say, "My track record speaks for itself".

340. You add disclaimers to your answers such as "This is kind of a silly example, but..."

341. When the interviewer asks what you can bring to the position you say, "Whatever you need".

342. You display incredible, yet doubtful, over the top confidence by saying, "I can show you how to turn this company around".

343. You repeat some phrases over and over without knowing it, such as "To be honest", or "That is a really good question".

344. You tell the interviewer, "I really shouldn't be telling you this...it's part of my company's proprietary intellectual property, or NDA, but..."

345. You use sentences that start with "One thing that really tics me off is...", and "I go ballistic when..." and "What really

makes me mad is...".

346. You don't take the time to ensure you know exactly how to pronounce the name of the company, their products or the interviewer's name.

347. You tell the interviewer how lucky they are that you are here to help them.

348. You emphasize how important being trained and having a mentor is to you, and they get the idea that you need lots of hand-holding.

" "

THE INTERVIEW GAME

"When an employment application asks who
is to be notified in case of emergency,
I always write, "A very good doctor"."

Anonymous

"You've achieved success in your field when
you don't know whether what you're
doing is work or play."

Warren Beatty

"You can follow your bliss, but there's got to
be some kind of pot of gold at the end
of all that bliss."

Bill Cole, MS, MA

579 BEHAVIORAL MISTAKES YOU MAKE DURING THE INTERVIEW

Now I REALLY know what you're thinking. How does this guy come up with so many mistakes? Is he making half of these up? Nope. Not at all. These are actual mistakes people make in actual interviews. The word behavioral just means what you do, rather than what you say. This is sometimes called non-verbal behavior. But it's just as strong as what comes out of your mouth. Maybe even more important. So read on and use this as a checklist for the actions you plan to avoid from here on out.

1. While you are on the premises of the company you are to interview with that day, during a break, or before or after your interview, you are overheard on your cell phone speaking with another potential employer.

2. You listen to a phone conversation the interviewer is having, and when he is done you comment on some aspect of it.

3. You arrive to the interview late, feel embarrassed, and proceed to immediately feel compelled to begin the interview, even though you could have asked to go to the restroom to tidy up, freshen up and regain your composure.

4. You profusely apologize to the interviewer each time you make a mistake, and they sense you come across as very needy or insecure.

5. You wear excessive or flashy jewelry to the interview.

6. You remove various articles of clothing in an effort to be more comfortable.

7. You place items on the conference table without asking permission.

8. When asked to send or bring basic items such as your resume and a cover letter, you add numerous items that were not requested.

9. In response to a question, instead of answering, you hand the interviewer a prepared, written statement.

10. You shrug your shoulders, or nod or shake your head instead of giving a verbal response.

11. You send a friend or family member to stand in for you at the interview.

12. You exude a pessimistic tone by hedging your enthusiasm and can-do spirit when asked if you can perform various job functions.

13. You smile or appear slightly amused regarding the interviewer's questions, but are not transparent about this, leaving the interviewer confused and wondering what you are thinking.

14. You bring work samples to the interview of your current employer's intellectual property.

15. At the end of a lunch or dinner interview you insist on paying. You also either leave no tip, a tiny tip or a huge tip.

16. You parse or rephrase the interviewer's questions to your liking.

17. As a result of the interviewer acting in what you perceive to be a hostile manner, you begin crying.

18. You have an odor from too much cologne or fragrance, strong food, or from smoking.

19. You show up with food and drink in your hands and are unable to shake hands properly.

20. You pick up an object in their office without being invited to do so.

21. You keep your iphone headphones wrapped around your neck during the interview.

22. You wear prescription sunglasses indoors.

23. You use your laptop to display some of your work, and have inappropriate items on the desktop or in the file, or on the website you use.

24. You hold a pen and/or click it as you speak.

25. You fail to make any eye contact with the interviewer.

26. As the interviewer is speaking, your eyes wander around the room.

27. You wear and flaunt expensive jewelry or a briefcase or pen to the interview, and that level of wealth display is not part of the industry culture in which you are interviewing.

28. The interviewer leaves his office and when he comes back you are speaking on your phone, or playing a game.

29. Since the interviewer appears to be the same age as you, and you discover you have some things in common, you drop your guard, relax and give a very casual interview.

30. You are so confident and excited that you'll get the job that you order business cards with the organization's name and logo, with your name on them and you hand them out at the interview.

31. To portray yourself as highly confident, you pretend to not be too interested in the position.

32. When being interviewed by a screener or lower level person, you act impatiently or indifferently, like they are the precursor to the "real" interviewer.

33. You dwell on how rough the economy and blame it on how hard it is to get a job in this competitive environment.

34. When asked how your job search is going, you cast yourself as a victim, and describe how hard everything is.

35. You sound like you are regurgitating book-learned strategies and techniques, and giving a book report, instead of describing your actual experience and how you made things happen.

36. Without knowing all the facts or history, you offer glib, fast, off the cuff and superficial solutions to problems the organization has been trying to solve for months.

37. You are asked about something with which you are not very familiar, yet you attempt to bluff your way through your answer.

38. You display a sarcastic sense of humor.

39. When you have a poor or inexperienced interviewer, you take charge and either begin telling them how to interview, or simply steer the interview in the direction you want to go, regardless of their desires.

40. You are aware that you are acting badly, or saying something wrong, yet the interviewer does not react, or say anything, so you think all is well.

41. You hire someone to write your resume, and you forget what is in it once in the interview.

42. You arrive to complete preliminary paperwork on a non-interview day in sloppy casual clothes. You do this because you believe paperwork is not part of the "interview".

43. Instead of making an appointment in advance, you just show up to the organization in hopes of having an

impromptu interview.

44. After the interviewer asks probing questions, or even attempts to prompt you in a helpful manner, you don't take the cue, and still give short answers with limited details.

45. In a series of interviews with different people at the same company, you tell them different answers to the same types of questions, or come across as a different person at each interview.

46. You claim you had the title of project manager when you only managed an occasional project.

47. You use the interview to prove how you can build personal relationships by becoming overly-friendly with the interviewer.

48. You fail to bring the requested, required documentation.

49. You don't read the literature the interviewer sends you, and then during the interview, you can't speak to it intelligently.

50.　You spend more time describing why you want to leave your current job, instead of why you want the job you are interviewing for.

51.　You knew what written materials you would need in the interview, yet you make the interviewer wait while you find them in your bag, and organize them so you can continue.

52.　Since you had very positive previous interviews and were encouraged by those interviewers by them hinting or saying that you are a strong candidate, you come to the final interviews with a sense of entitlement.

53.　Since you were told by a previous interviewer in the company that the final interview is to merely be a formality, or a casual opportunity for you to meet the team, you relax and let down your guard, and assume you have the job.

54.　You respond to a job posting that is far beyond your level of experience.

55.　You are so afraid of coming across as arrogant and as a braggart that you undersell yourself and force the interviewer to pull data out of you.

56. You fail to appreciate or respect something the interviewer deems to be important.

57. You act judgmental, about anything.

58. You have an air of being contrarian, whereby you tend to be oppositional, and take the opposing views of the interviewer.

59. You are so relaxed, and act so casually in the interview that they believe you really don't care about the position, and they suspect that you are there "practicing your interview skills".

60. You don't use please and thank you.

61. You don't show appreciation for the interviewer's time.

62. You display impatience.

63. You decide to close your eyes while you are waiting for the interviewer, and fall asleep.

64. You are falsely modest even though you have strong accomplishments.

65. The interviewer calls you by the wrong name, or forgets your name, and you are observably miffed.

66. You bring your personal photo album to share.

67. You bring the interviewer a gift in order to ingratiate them.

68. You secretly attempt to record the interview.

69. You are visibly irritated and miffed at having to go through the interview process since you believe "They should know I want the job, since I applied and showed up", and "Why do I need to answer such obvious questions? Don't they know I want to be part of their company?", and "I hate jumping through all their stupid hoops and playing this dumb interview game".

70. The interviewer shares some personal Information, some grievances, some pet peeves or some irritations with you and asks for you (or strongly hints) to

do the same, and you oblige.

71.   The interviewer encourages you to be "truly candid" about what you did not like about your previous company or boss, and you oblige.

72.   The interviewer asks you questions that were clearly on the application, and you are observably miffed having to answer them again.

73.   The interviewer asks you questions that were asked by previous interviewers at their company, and you are observably miffed having to answer them again.

74.   You give an answer that does not match the question.

75.   The interviewer insults your background, previous employer, school, or other areas in your profile, and you become observably irritated, flustered, angry, or emotional.

76.   You don't follow directions if you're given a test, or asked to perform a demonstration.

77. You attempt to come across at the same experience level as the senior interviewer, when you are not.

78. You use big words and obtuse phrases in an effort to impress the interviewer.

79. You show interest in a different department within the company or different career paths altogether.

80. You engage in self-sabotage by down-playing yourself or underselling yourself.

81. After the interviewer talks about himself or the company, you display an urgency to tell them about yourself.

82. You make a mistake on an answer and let it show that you are upset about it.

83. The interviewer says they did not read your resume, and you are observably miffed.

84. As you see the interviewer relax and become more casual, you let your guard down and act that way also.

85. You had too much coffee and are talking a mile a minute, and acting jumpy.

86. You try to be funny and clever.

87. You are eating or chewing anything, in the lobby or in the interview room.

88. The interviewer takes or makes a phone call in the middle of the interview, and while you are waiting, you act inappropriately.

89. The interviewer makes or takes a phone call for some period of time, making you wait, and you are observably miffed during and after the call.

90. You give the interviewer unsolicited advice.

91. You try to "buddy up" or become too friendly with the interviewer.

92. While Generation Xers and baby boomers have a home face, a friend face, and a business face, you have the same face with everyone you meet-

informal and sociable.

93. You send out signals that say "What's in it for me?" instead of "Here's what I can do for you".

94. When asked if you have an extra copy of your resume, you say yes, and pull out a crumpled, stained copy to hand the interviewer.

95. You let it be known that your need for work-life balance is more important than the work that has to be accomplished.

96. You look at the floor as you are thinking about an answer, making you look like you are making lying or something up.

97. You offer to do a special personal favor for the interviewer some time, in an effort to ingratiate yourself with him.

98. When the company goes to check you out on social media, you have inappropriate content or pictures posted.

99. In a panel interview you give more attention to some interviewers than others.

100. You do so much research on the interviewer, and share this data during the interview, they feel like they are being stalked.

101. You insult people who went to a "state school", since you went to a prestigious university, not knowing the interviewer went to a state school.

102. The interviewer introduces himself using his title (Doctor, Captain, Reverend, Dean, etc) and you leave these off as you address him.

103. You offer suggestions of how to change their company without being asked.

104. You make a comment about the interviewer's appearance, office, car, or anything else.

105. You ask the interviewer confidential and proprietary information about their company because "you are curious".

106. The interviewer says something you disagree with and you take umbrage, and are visibly miffed.

107. You are too honest and overly transparent in disclosing a weakness or dislike.

108. You yawn or stretch or act tired at any time during the interview.

109. You make statements that show you are intolerant of other people's viewpoints and values.

110. You refuse to answer a certain question, because you think it's irrelevant.

111. If the interviewer is a loud, fast speaking individual, or a slow, soft speaking individual, you don't adjust your own speaking speed and volume to match their style.

112. You cry in response to a question, criticism or reaction from the interviewer.

113. The interviewer cannot tell if you are listening to them or not, because you sit very still and very silently, without providing any feedback or signs to them that you are indeed with them.

114. Your friend comes in from the lobby unannounced and asks the interviewer "How much longer will this be"?

115. The interviewer misstates facts about your record, and you are visibly miffed.

116. The interviewer states that they lost your resume, and asks if you have another for them, and you are visibly miffed.

117. The interviewer criticizes your answers and you react with visible defens-iveness or emotionality.

118. The interviewer asks illegal or borderline illegal questions and you react indignantly.

119. The interviewer asks very basic questions for your level of experience, and you display impatience or disapproval.

120. The interviewer uses the active listening technique of paraphrasing back to you what you just said, but they get it wrong, and you are visibly miffed that you believe "they are not listening".

121. The interviewer says "Are you sure you don't want to change your answer?", and you are observably miffed or flustered.

122. The interviewer provides unclear or inaccurate instructions for a task or demonstration you will be doing, yet you move ahead with it, hoping to fake it.

123. Upon learning that the interviewer likes golf or another sport, you frame all your answers using golf language and examples or sports language and examples.

124. Your interview philosophy and strategy is to just answer everything as honestly as possible, and you say things that are too honest with items that should not be disclosed.

125. You have distracting, noisy jewelry or clashing colors in your outfit.

126. You are interviewed in a less than ideal room setting and are visibly irritated about it.

127. Because you think you know the question the interviewer is asking, you "hurry him along" by displaying impatience.

128. You wear an outfit that does not match what people in their organization wear.

129. You don't have a fresh haircut, shave, shower and all else that goes with presenting yourself in a professional manner.

130. You comment on how other people "look" at their organization.

131. You wear cologne or perfume that is overpowering.

132. Your shoes are not shined.

133. You wear loafers instead of lace shoes to a more formal interview.

134. You wear sneakers, flip-slops or casual shoes to a more formal interview.

135. You don't "match your leathers". That is, you have a brown belt, black shoes and red watch band, rather than making them all one color.

136. You chew gum or suck on candy during the interview.

137. You tell the interviewer the room is hot and you take off numerous items of clothing to get more comfortable.

138. The briefcase or valise you carry is old, worn or dirty.

139. You have dirty or soiled clothing.

140. You don't wear socks.

141. You don't wear a belt.

142. You don't comb your hair or shave properly.

143. Without asking if it's OK, you take out your written materials or other items and display them on the table.

144. Without asking if it's OK, you stand up and conduct part or all of the interview standing.

145. Without asking if it's OK, you check your cell phone for messages.

146. Without asking if it's OK, you respond to a text.

147. Without asking if it's OK, you take an incoming call.

148. Without asking if it's OK, you stand up, walk out, saying you need to use the bathroom.

149. Without asking if it's OK, you pick up an item on the interviewer's desk and begin playing with it.

150. Without asking if it's OK, you turn on your computer and display a PowerPoint you developed.

151. Without asking if it's OK, you walk up to the whiteboard and begin using it.

152. Without asking if it's OK, you get up and adjust the thermostat in the room to fix the temperature.

153. Without asking if it's OK, you announce that you have a series of questions you'd like the interviewer to answer.

154. Without asking if it's OK, you bring in a video camera and turn it on.

155. Without asking if it's OK, you pull out your cell phone and begin recording.

156. Without asking if it's OK, you pull out a notebook and begin to write down everything the interviewer says. You ask them to repeat themselves.

157. You look out the window because you're bored with the questioning.

158. You yawn and don't attempt to cover it up or to apologize.

159. You ask how much longer the interview will take, saying you have another

interview at a different organization.

160. You ask the interviewer for advice about a non-work related life issue.

161. You ask the interviewer to compare their job offering with their competitor, with whom you are also interviewing.

162. When the interviewer asks if you have any questions you say no.

163. When the interviewer asks if you have any questions you say the previous interviewer answered them all.

164. When the interviewer asks if you have any questions you say the tour guide covered all your questions.

165. When the interviewer asks if you have any questions you say you found all you need to know on the organization's website.

166. When the interviewer asks if you have any questions you only ask one or two.

167. When the interviewer asks if you have any questions you say, "Finally! My

turn!"

168. You lean on the table or the side of your chair.

169. You swivel and rock in your chair.

170. You rock your leg, twiddle your fingers or make other distracting mannerisms.

171. You sit too close or too far back from the table.

172. When you comment on photos or objects in the interviewer's office, you attempt to "one-up" them or put them down.

173. When the interviewer becomes very relaxed and casual, you do also, and look unprofessional.

174. You leave notifications active on your cell phone or computer, and they alert during the interview.

175. You tell the interviewer you are expecting an important phone call, and to please hurry up.

176. You are far too honest and disclose things you should not say.

177. Your answers are far too short or far too long.

178. You lose the connection between you and the interviewer and don't realize it, and don't do anything to correct it.

179. You don't pay attention to rapport.

180. When asked to name something you dislike about your current or previous boss and company, you become very enthusiastic about it and carry on with many items you dislike.

181. The interviewer asks one of those crazy nonsense questions and you take offense, saying it's irrelevant to the job.

182. You fumble with your papers and pen.

183. The interviewer catches you in a lie or inconsistency.

184. You become argumentative.

185. The interviewer challenges your answer and you take offence.

186. You laugh nervously when you are afraid.

187. You tell the interviewer you can't understand them with their accent.

188. You don't actually answer the question because you're not listening accurately.

189. You don't make good eye contact with the interviewer.

190. You are uncomfortable making small talk, so you don't even try to do so.

191. The interviewer cuts you off and you show your irritation.

192. The interviewer asks an illegal question and you berate them.

193. If the interview is delayed or disrupted, you display irritation.

194. Because you don't like bragging about yourself, you don't sell yourself in any way at all.

195. You hope the interviewer likes you and thinks you are a fit for the job, and instead you don't tell them you want the job.

196. You become uncomfortable if there is any degree of silence, so you talk to fill it.

197. You ramble on and never seem to end an answer properly.

198. You have red flags in your past and you don't have cohesive stories to explain them.

199. When the interviewer asks about one of your red flags you over-explain it, and thereby appear like you are trying to cover something up.

200. When you are asked to demonstrate something you become miffed.

201. You don't match your vocal volume to the interviewer.

202. You are unable to identify, and answer trick questions.

203. The interviewer seems disengaged, and you ask if they are bored.

204. You make a mistake and beat yourself up over it in your mind.

205. You use filler words too much, as such as "like", "you know", etc.

206. You have itchy skin and continuously scratch it, but don't tell the interviewer about your condition.

207. You tell the interviewer how nervous you are.

208. The interviewer used words you don't know and you say they are trying to put you down.

209. You virtually sit on your hands and don't use them at all.

210. You use your hands too much.

211. You don't know how to analyze the personality of the interviewer.

212. You don't know how to do research on the organization.

213. You research the interviewer but disclose you know too much about their personal life.

214. You pull out notes and tell the interviewer you have a bad memory.

215. You speak in a monotone voice.

216. You run your sentences together.

217. You speak too fast or too slow.

218. You wait far too long before beginning your answers.

219. You trail your voice of at the end of sentences.

220. Your voice has the "vocal fry" effect where you growl at the end of sentences and answers.

221. You don't wrap up or summarize your answers, so you sound abrupt to the interviewer.

222. You don't know how to gracefully stall to buy time.

223. You don't know how to "save an answer" if you make a mistake.

224. You don't have a personal branding statement and strategy.

225. You don't review the job or school prospectus to help you precisely target your application and candidacy to it, both in writing and in the interview.

226. You don't match your strengths, talents, skills, values and goals to be able to match your unique abilities to what the school or job is seeking.

227. You don't arrange for mock interview practice simulation sessions, to make them feel exactly like the "real thing" so you can "practice to the interview", so there are no surprises.

228. You don't know how to counter and overcome objections an interviewer may have about you.

229. You don't have strategies for handling an interviewer who is attempting to intimidate you.

230. You don't know how to manage the wide variety of interview types-panel, group, serial, dining, case study, behavioral, scenario, MMI and others.

231. You don't ask key clarifying and uncovering questions early in the interview so you can target the rest of your interview remarks to what the interviewer is "really seeking".

232. You don't have a system for deciphering and delivering answers to scenario-based questions.

233. You don't know what to do and say if you lose your place in the middle of an answer.

234. You don't know when to make eye contact, and when not to.

235. You don't know how to deal with "uncomfortable silences" in an interview so they're no longer uncomfortable.

236. You don't know how to display passion and enthusiasm to the interviewer (even if that is not your natural personality style).

237. You don't arrange mock interview time so that feels exactly like the "real interview" you will soon have, so you can work out any "sticking points" in advance.

238. You don't know how to think on your feet, so you can come up with answers to questions you never even thought about before.

239. You don't know how to overcome any shyness you may have, so you can show the interviewer your best qualities and eliminate your self-consciousness.

240. You don't know how to evaluate the "job fit" and the "cultural fit" of the position.

241. You don't know how to assess the job offer itself so you know if the salary and

benefits package is what you want.

242. You don't know how to use "acting techniques" so you can show the proper emotions, hand gestures and body language that match your stories.

243. You don't know how to handle embarrassing questions or rude comments the interviewer may make, and still stay on track with your answers.

244. You don't know how to make adjustments to your answers if the interviewer makes changes to the interview format at the last moment.

245. You don't know how to navigate group interviews so you can stand out.

246. You don't know how to avoid using trite cliches and over-used words and phrases so your answers sound original and fresh.

247. You don't know how to understand your knowledge, skills, and abilities (KSA's) as they specifically relate to the exact job announcement, and to craft short, crisp, and clear KSA essays.

248. You don't know how to identify specific job requirements on the job announcement such as evaluation factors, rating factors, knowledge, abilities, job elements, skills, and other characteristics, or quality ranking factors, and match your capabilities to these.

249. You don't know how to understand what the job announcement is specifically asking for, and guide you in matching your background to that so the fit is perfect.

250. You don't know how to craft excellent case studies from your experience.

251. You don't know how to tell great, compelling success stories about yourself.

252. You don't know how to respond to the hostile interviewer statement, "You're not what we're looking for in a candidate".

253. You don't know how to use "get back on track techniques" to employ if you notice the interviewer is not listening to you.

254. You don't know the different ways you can respond if the interviewer asks you an illegal question.

255. You don't know how the strategies for handling the difference between in-person, Skype and phone interview approaches to interviewing.

256. You don't know about salary and package negotiation strategies.

257. You don't know how to analyze the interviewer in real-time so you can figure them out enough to craft your answers to what they expect.

258. You don't know how to use practice strategies so you can remember your stories and other answers.

259. You don't know how to prepare for, remain calm, and perform well in the "stress or hostile interview".

260. You don't know how to become aware of, and remove the various tics and repetitive physical mannerisms you have that are negatively perceived by interviewers.

261. You don't know how to control your nervous energy so your nervous tics and stress reactions are hidden from the interviewer.

262. You don't know how to correctly speak with your hands so you appear more energetic, passionate and congruent.

263. You don't know the secrets of how to identify "trick questions" so you can remain calm, take your time and give the "real answer they are looking for", not the fake one.

264. You don't know how to adapt your tone to that of the interviewer so you build rapport and match their level of formality.

265. You don't know your special uniqueness as a person so you can tell the interviewer why you are the ideal person they should choose.

266. You don't know how to find and to ask intelligent, unique questions so you can show how interested you are in the position.

267. You don't know how to gracefully handle any disruptions, tricks or curveballs that may arise.

268. You don't have a system for gaining "control of the clock" in the interview process from the outset so you can take your time, go at a comfortable pace, and never feel rushed by the interviewer.

269. You don't know how to artfully start a poor answer over from the beginning, or amend it at any time later.

270. You don't know how to gracefully announce yourself to the lobby receptionist and what to do while you are waiting.

271. You don't know how to read the "cues and vibes" of an interview, so you can tell if things are going well or not, and how to adjust if they are not.

272. You don't know how to answer a question you have absolutely no idea how to answer.

273. You don't know how to use memory tricks so you can organize and recall

your answers easily.

274. You don't know ways to answer "the fantasy, puzzle, brain-teaser or silly questions" interviewers like to ask.

275. You don't know how to reframe the interviewer's negative premise in their question into a positive answer.

276. You don't know how to practice so you can limit stammering and stuttering in your answers.

277. You don't know how to craft a solid, believable answer to the red flags in your resume or CV around poor grades, test scores, gaps, poor reviews or firings.

278. You don't know how to use advanced communication techniques on confusing multi-part questions so you can organize them in your mind and deliver a crisp, clear response.

279. You don't know ways to calmly withstand and tactfully counter an interviewer who is argumentative and confrontational.

280. You don't know how to properly understand the question, even from an interviewer who has a difficult accent, or who asks poorly-worded questions.

281. You don't know how to handle an inter-viewer who cuts you off mid-sentence.

282. You don't know how to cover up any mistake you might make, so you can keep moving on with your answer.

283. You don't know how to non-arrogantly "brag about yourself", even if you hate to "talk about yourself", so you sell yourself to the interviewer.

284. You don't know how to use small talk (even if you are shy and even if you dislike small talk).

285. You don't know how to handle questions where they ask you to demonstrate something.

286. You don't know how to "save a bad interview" that you thought was a lost cause.

287. You don't know how to craft strategies and positioning statements if you are changing careers or industries.

288. You don't know how to recover during an interview if you begin to blank out, lose your place, suffer a memory lapse or start an answer the wrong way.

289. You don't know how to remove a negative attitude and mental blocks about interviewing, so you can remain positive.

290. You don't know how to craft a special job hunt strategy if you are over 50 years of age.

291. You don't know how to overcome the fear of success, and the fear of failure.

292. You don't know how to have natural eye contact and facial expressions.

293. You don't know how to time your answers so they're not too short or too long.

294. You don't know what to say if the interviewer repeats a question identically.

295. You don't know how and when to ask questions of the interviewer.

296. You don't know how to show the perfect fit between your background and capabilities and what the interviewer is seeking.

297. You don't know how to demonstrate you are listening so the interviewer feels engaged with you.

298. You don't know how to answer confidently, but so you don't come across as being arrogant or cocky.

299. You don't know how to watch for the signs that you may be coming on too strong or "over-selling yourself" and thereby alienating the interviewer.

300. You don't know how to do research on the company or school so you have plenty of customized questions to ask, and so you stand out as a person who goes the extra mile, and who is an amazing researcher.

301. You don't know organizational methods that stop you from talking about irrelevant material and instead, help

you target the most important details in your answers.

302. You don't know how to craft a personalized, custom final statement that tells the interviewer what you will do for them, how much you want the position, and that will leave them with a highly positive impression of you.

303. You don't know how to remain professional, yet warm and friendly.

304. You don't know what to say if you've been fired so the interviewer does not hold it against you.

305. You don't know how to avoid falling for critical salary negotiation traps.

306. You don't know how to "control the interview" without coming across as controlling or manipulative.

307. You don't know how to show your passion for the position, without appearing to be needy.

308. You don't know how to describe what you do in terms of accomplishments,

not just activities or tasks.

309. You don't know how to ask key questions early in the interview that gives you information as to what is really important to the interviewer, and therefore of how to conduct the rest of the interview.

310. You don't know how to build rapport with the interviewer without becoming too personal, or unprofessional.

311. You don't know how to answer the question "Why do you want to work for our company?" so that your answers are focused on how you can benefit the company, instead of what you want out of the job.

312. You don't know how to diplomatically answer an interruption from the interviewer and gracefully get back on track.

313. You don't know when to be fully disclosing, and when to hold back some information.

314. You don't know how to handle personal, illegal, or borderline illegal questions with tact and diplomacy so the interviewer is not put off.

315. You don't have a plan for recovering with the interviewer after a poor interview (using email and the telephone) so that you may still have a chance.

316. You don't know how to "read the interviewer" in terms of their personality values, style and body language so you can match your presentation to their sensibilities.

317. You don't know how to let go of errors you make in the interview so you can stay present and on track.

318. You don't know how to use a positioning statement or banner statement to frame each answer so it makes more sense to the interviewer.

319. You don't know how to handle, repeat, irrelevant or off-topic questions with tact.

320. You don't know techniques to use when the interviewer uses terms or phrases you don't understand, so you can still answer the question.

321. You don't know how to handle the dreaded interviewer question they may ask after you give an answer, "Do you want to change your answer?, or, "Is that your final answer", or "Is that your best answer"?.

322. You don't know how to turn a one-way interview into a collegial back and forth conversation.

323. You don't know about the art of persuasion skills to make yourself more convincing.

324. You don't know how to stop self-criticism and to stop second-guessing yourself when you answer.

325. You don't know how to handle disruptions, surprises and unusual situations in an interview and still stay on track.

326. You don't know techniques for controlling the clock, so you gain extra time to think if your mind goes blank.

327. You don't know the "active listening method" which will enable you to precisely identify and understand the "real question" the interviewer is asking, so you don't fall for their tricks and traps.

328. You don't know how to find unique and intelligent questions to ask of the interviewer.

329. You don't know how to state that you are very interested in the position, without coming across as needy or desperate.

330. You don't know how to come across as friendly and professional, even if you are quiet, shy and reserved.

331. You don't know how to analyze a job prospectus so you can craft your message to fit it to a "T".

332. You don't know how to "figure out the interviewer" so you can create better

rapport and connection with them.

333. You don't understand "Emotional Intelligence" (EI, or EQ), and to use your emotional intelligence skills to read the interviewer and adapt your answers to that person.

334. You don't know how to look for the signals and cues that tell you that your answers are going on too long.

335. You don't know when to ask, and when to avoid asking these pointed questions: "Do you have any concerns about my candidacy?" or, "Is there anything holding you back from offering me this position?"

336. You don't know how to show the interviewer how your work is a kind of life mission, a dedicated passion and not just a job.

337. You don't know ways to ask questions so you can find the company's "pain" or challenges and tell them how you can take their pain away.

338. You don't know how to stop fidgeting with your jewelry, glasses, hands or pen.

339. You don't know what to do when the interviewer says "This is off the record". (There is no such thing as "off the record".)

340. You don't know how to avoid devolving into irrelevant personal data when you answer questions, and to keep the tone business-like and professional.

341. You don't know how to realistically describe the shortcomings of previous bosses and companies when asked, without sounding negative and critical.

342. You don't know how to use deep listening skills so you don't answer the question "you think the interviewer asked", but instead to be able listen carefully to answer the real question.

343. You don't know how to use techniques to stall gracefully while you think of what to say.

344. You don't know how to read the body language of the interviewer so you can adjust your message to them and stay engaged.

345. You don't know how to behave at an interview conducted over breakfast, lunch or dinner, or at an entertainment or sporting event.

346. You don't know how to show your interest in the position and passion for the field, even if you are an introvert and quiet and shy.

347. You don't know how to engage in small talk as you walk to the interview room with the guide or interviewer, so you can create rapport, and calm your nerves.

348. You don't know the best ways to answer the question, "Why did you leave each position?", so that there is absolutely no question in the interviewer's mind that you left for the right reasons, and under the most ideal circumstances.

349. You don't know how to answer the question, "Explain the gap in employment you have here", such that they will be completely satisfied and never ask you again.

350. You don't know how to answer questions known as puzzle questions,

brain teasers, fantasy questions or nonsense questions.

351. You don't know how to turn what feels like an interrogation into a collegial, interesting conversation.

352. You don't know how to tell the interviewer compelling reasons why you want to work for them specifically, rather than having generic things to say.

353. You don't know how to understand what the interviewer wants from a candidate, so you can tailor your answers to that.

354. You don't know what things not to say before and after each answer, so your answers are complete, yet streamlined.

355. You don't know how to appear more confident, even if you don't feel very confident at the time.

356. You don't know how to answer concisely so you don't ramble or endlessly search for the "right thing to say".

357. You don't know how to understand and correctly answer complex and multipart questions.

358. You don't know how to avoid going off on tangents and irrelevant topics in your answers.

359. You don't know how to approach case-study questions.

360. You don't know stress management techniques so you stay centered, calm and focused.

361. You don't know how to be mentally tough in an interview.

362. You don't know how to recover if you lose your place on an answer.

363. You don't know how to properly handle the resume questions such as: Why is there a gap? Why did you jump around so much? Aren't you overqualified? Did you get fired?

364. You don't know what to do if the interviewer is rude, cuts you off, or otherwise acts badly.

365. You don't know methods for "selling yourself" without sounding like you are bragging.

366. You don't know what to say if you have no idea whatsoever how to answer the question.

367. You don't know methods for handling an interviewer who is confrontational or hostile.

368. You don't know have memory systems for remembering what you want to say.

369. You don't know the specific times when you should take notes or use materials or handouts you brought with you to the interview.

370. You don't know what do if the interviewer changes the interview style or format on you at the last moment.

371. You don't know how to avoid the incorrect ways to practice for an interview, and the right ways to practice so you have good recall and sound natural.

372. You don't know how to use silence in an interview to your advantage.

373. You don't know when and when not to use humor in an interview.

374. You don't know how to show your passion and enthusiasm for the job, even if you don't feel that way at the time.

375. You don't know how to use your hands so they display energy, poise and confidence.

376. You don't know how to break down, organize and answer multipart questions.

377. You give the interviewer too much respect in your own mind, and you then act intimidated.

378. You fail to assess and match the formality level of situation.

379. You take the interview too seriously and are unable to smile at all, when appropriate.

380. You don't memorize your opening and closing statements, to allay nerves, which are sure to be there at those times.

381. You wait in fear hoping the interviewer won't attack you with one of your red flags, rather than bringing it up first so you can control the narrative.

382. You behave the same in a group interview as you do in a 1-1 interview.

383. You answer some questions instantly, causing an answer you pause on to seem like an eternity.

384. You apologize for yourself and your accomplishments.

385. You don't tell the interviewer directly that you want the job.

386. You are an executive and you say "job" instead of role, position or opportunity.

387. You use sexist, genderist, classist, ageist language.

388. You use inappropriate slang and jargon.

389. You use foreign language phrases to try and impress the interviewer.

390. Your delivery seems rehearsed and memorized.

391. You are afraid to disagree with the interviewer.

392. If you have a differing opinion than the interviewer, you say so, but you do not use much diplomacy.

393. You allow the interviewer to get off-track and ask questions not pertinent to the job.

394. When the small talk is flowing, you get over-eager and butt in to change the subject so you can talk about your capabilities for the job.

395. After every question, you say to the interviewer, "That's a good question", or "I'm glad you asked me that question".

396. You use all data and no stories in your answers.

397. You use all stories and no data in your answers.

398. You don't clarify poorly-worded questions from the interviewer.

399. You react defensively to probing questions.

400. You read an interview book that contained answers, and your answers sound just like they came out of that book.

401. You don't personalize your answers with stories and examples.

402. Your answers are not well-organized, so the interviewer can't follow you.

403. When the interviewer loses connection with you, you believe they are just tired, not that you are boring, off-target, or rambling.

404. You are overly passive and fail to ask questions as you go.

405. You don't know how to sell yourself.

406. You hope the interviewer knows how much you want the job, but you don't tell them this.

407. You fail to show the fit of your abilities to the position.

408. You discuss religion, politics, personal issues or other sensitive topics.

409. You second-guess yourself on answers.

410. You appear to be needy and almost begging for the job.

411. You slouch and sink into the chair.

412. You gesture with one hand only.

413. You don't practice answers, because you're afraid they'll sound stilted and rehearsed in the interview.

414. You think that the less you craft and plan your answers, the less you'll have to remember under pressure.

415. You think if you "brag about yourself" the interviewer will view you as an

arrogant egomaniac, so you don't even try to sell yourself at all.

416. You trust the interviewer to run the interview, and you just sit there and do whatever they want you to.

417. You take all the interviewer's questions at face value, and you don't attempt to clarify them.

418. You rarely paraphrase the question before you answer.

419. When you don't understand the question, you simply ask the interviewer to repeat the question, without displaying that you indeed hear it correctly.

420. You believe it's a mistake to admit a true weakness, and that it's better to make one up, or to say you really don't have any.

421. You answer immediately after the question is posed, because you believe if you take time to think, the interviewer will think you don't know what I'm doing, so you rush.

422. If you don't understand a question, a term or a phrase in a question, you pretend to grasp it, and attempt an answer, so you look like you know what you're doing.

423. If you ask for clarification of the question, you believe the interviewer will think you're either not listening, or not very knowledgeable.

424. If you reframe, paraphrase or question the interviewer's assumptions in their question, you believe the interviewer will think you're confronting them, or that you don't like their question.

425. If the interviewer asks you the same question twice, you simply answer it again, because you think that if you point out that they already asked it, that will just embarrass the interviewer, and they'll dislike you.

426. You believe you must do a virtually flawless job to impress the interviewer.

427. You don't believe you need to hold an actual "mock interview" ahead of time to prepare.

428. Because you don't want to appear fake and overly formal, you use your "daily street language" and slang you use with your friends.

429. If the interviewer wants you to say negative things about your boss or company, you just answer negatively so you don't rock the boat and look disagreeable to the interviewer.

430. If the interviewer asks one of those silly brainteaser, puzzle, fantasy type questions, you say you don't like those questions, and ask for a new question, because you don't see their relevance to the interview.

431. You think it will be sufficient to read over a few questions the morning of the interview, and think about what you'd say, instead of making interview preparation an ongoing project.

432. You think that good eye contact is never taking your eyes off the interviewer.

433. You hope and assume the interviewer knows how much you want the position, so you don't come right out

and say it.

434. You don't know what Emotional Intelligence skills are, and why they are important.

435. You believe that if you alter your behavior to fit another person's needs, you're being fake.

436. Your answers are superficial, lack detail, incomplete and too short.

437. You take questions too literally and miss nuance and the invitation to expand your answer.

438. Your answers don't answer the actual question posed.

439. You're not able to figure out what your "special sauce" is, or what makes you unique, compared to all the other candidates.

440. You're uncomfortable with the social aspects of meeting new people, and the interviewer picks up on that, and perceives you as not fitting in to their culture.

441. You relied on getting answers from your friends and on-line but they're too commonplace, trite, obvious and generic, and the interviewer senses this, and realizes you're not the unique candidate they seek.

442. You are understandably anxious about doing well in the interview, but you unfortunately "try too hard to impress" and you block yourself from being sharp mentally, you forget what you wanted to say, or you come across as stiff or uptight to the interviewer.

443. You don't know how to handle the wide variety of interview types: panel, group, serial, dining, case study, behavioral, scenario, MMI and others.

444. You look away from the interviewer when you are thinking, and even often when you are thinking as you speak.

445. You are very intellectual, and you have a great academic mind, but unfortunately, your heavily cognitive style comes across as sterile, distant and remote, and the interviewer perceives you as having no enthusiasm.

446. You don't know how to handle direct, probing or challenging questions the interviewer may pose, and still stay on track with your answers.

447. You don't know how to gain "control of the clock" in the interview from the outset so you can take your time, go at a comfortable pace, and never feel rushed by the interviewer.

448. You don't know the specific techniques for how to recover during an interview if you begin to blank out, lose your place, suffer a memory lapse or start an answer the wrong way.

449. You don't know how to craft a personalized, custom final statement that tells the interviewer what you will do for them, how much you want to join their organization, that will leave them with a highly positive impression of you.

450. You don't know any techniques to stall gracefully while you think of what to say with difficult questions. Instead, you feel rushed, and the interviewer views you as someone who makes answers up as they go.

451. You hope the interviewer knows how much you like their organization, but you never come out and actually say that. You leave and the interviewer thinks, "That person is nice, but they really aren't very interested in us, so we're not very interested in them either."

452. You believe your answers are good, but since you've never tested them with either a professional interview coach or real live interviewer, you're just taking a stab in the dark.

453. You are unable to identify the numerous counterintuitive "trick questions" that are contained in every interview.

454. You don't answer concisely, and instead ramble on endlessly in search of the "right thing to say".

455. You are not very good at "thinking on your feet" when you are asked questions you have not rehearsed.

456. You have not practiced or thought through what you would say to the core set of 15 or so most common interview questions, so you dread that they may

be asked, and this anxiety ruins your energy, focus and ability to be present in the interview.

457. You rehearsed your answers all right, but you did so only in your head. Then when you begin speaking at the real interview, you're not used to the sound of your own voice, you don't enunciate some words well, and you stutter or stammer.

458. You don't know the etiquette, the do's and don'ts, and the social cues of how to behave in the interview. This makes you feel ill at ease, and this comes across to the interviewer as a lack of rapport.

459. You are not used to having someone challenge your answers. When the interviewer probes and asks follow up questions, you feel attacked and don't know how to respond.

460. You go off on tangents and irrelevant topics in your answers.

461. You're a nice person, but the interviewer never gets to see that in you because you rarely smile due to

your nerves.

462. If the interview gets to the hostile or stress level, where the interviewer says things like, "I don't like your answer", or "Do you want to change that answer?", you have no idea what to say.

463. You either speak too little or too much, but you don't know how to strike a good ratio of the two.

464. You don't know how to read the signals that tell you that the interview is going well, or badly.

465. You don't adjust and ask the interviewer questions if they rarely have follow up questions.

466. You avoid practicing the questions that scare you.

467. You avoid doing the hard work of crafting great answers, and instead settle for the obvious, feel good, top of mind answers.

468. You avoid replicating the actual interview conditions, by not wearing the

same clothes you will use, sitting in similar chairs, etc., and when the actual interview arrives, you feel out of your element.

469. You try to "force it to happen" instead of "letting it happen".

470. You characterize what you will do for the organization as just a job, not as you being on a mission or as having a calling.

471. You don't find the organization's "pain" so you can show how you can take that away.

472. You look at your watch, phone or the wall clock in the interview, rather than letting the interviewer handle the time.

473. You ask about pay, benefits, vacation and other non-essentials in the initial interview.

474. You devolve into irrelevant personal data when you answer questions.

475. Your body language does not match what your words are saying.

476. You assume you know what the interviewer's question will be, so you begin to formulate your answer as they ask it, and when the question turns out not to be what you thought, you give the wrong answer.

477. You swivel your chair mindlessly.

478. You don't face the interviewer in your chair directly, and instead look at him from the side.

479. You cover your mouth with your hands as you speak.

480. In an effort to appear compliant and agreeable, you sit very still in your chair for long periods of time.

481. You give such short answers that the interviewer is forced to pull answers out of you with obvious follow-up questions.

482. You attempt to tell the interviewer you want the job too soon.

483. You have incongruence between your body language and words.

484. You assume you have the job, and begin phrasing your conversation as if you are already on the team.

485. The interviewer has made you an offer and you continue to "sell".

486. You deliver your answers in a "too slick to be true" manner.

487. You act like a know-it-all and display arrogance and ego.

488. You contradict yourself on facts, dates or places.

489. You don't give both "heart" and "head" answers.

490. When the interviewer raises a concern, you take it as a sign that you won't get the job, and mentally give up.

491. When the interviewer uses small talk, you try to one-up or top them with what you do.

492. When asked for your resume, you have to fumble to find it.

493. When asked to produce some papers and you can't quickly find them, you overtly appear upset about it.

494. You don't use any personal disclosure as to what you think and how you feel, so the interviewer really does not get to know who you are.

495. You show little or no curiosity in the interviewer when he talks about issues important to him.

496. You compliment the interviewer on how they look.

497. You compliment the interviewer in such a way they feel you are "kissing up" to them.

498. The interviewer makes a comment about something inconsequential, and you correct them, making them wrong.

499. You disclose a confidentiality or private matter that you should not.

500. You finish the interviewer's sentences.

501. You're argumentative and oppositional.

502. You tell the interviewer what they "should do" by moralizing or lecturing them.

503. You ask questions of the interviewer that shows you don't trust what they tell you.

504. When asked a fantasy, silly or nonsensical question, you either take offense, and you say you don't answer irrelevant questions, or you take it too seriously.

505. You answer a yes or no question with a long story or explanation with lots of details, and finally, only at the every end, do you say yes or no.

506. If the interviewer cuts you off repeatedly, you just allow that to happen, instead of showing that you will finish what you were saying.

507. You miss or ignore the interviewer's cues that he is trying to ask you something.

508. You tap, spin or play with your pen, or other object.

509. You touch your face or hair often.

510. You cover your mouth when you are embarrassed or unsure of what you're saying.

511. You tell the interviewer that you "overuse your hands" when you talk, and say that you are going to sit on them during the interview so you can keep them under control.

512. You use charm and personality to impress the interviewer.

513. You actually flirt with the interviewer.

514. You play inspiring music on your phone to impress the interviewer.

515. Because you believe that asking questions is a mark of weakness, you don't ask any.

516. Because you believe that asking questions shows you aren't prepared, you don't ask any.

517. You act like the interviewer is a long-lost buddy.

518. You don't actually demonstrate to the interviewer that you are indeed listening.

519. The interviewer says you are not listening and you begin arguing, insisting that you are listening.

520. You are so nervous that you actually get tears in your eyes.

521. When the interviewer challenges you or acts in a hostile manner, you shut down emotionally.

522. You leave the interview without telling the interviewer the most important things about you, because those questions were not asked.

523. You have a very weak handshake.

524. You come across as if you are entitled and expect a lot that others don't get.

525. You use trite, hackneyed and all-too-common buzz words such as "deep dive", paradigm and others.

526. In arranging the interview, you whine, complain or are concerned about the time, the day, the traffic, the parking, the walk to the building and all else.

527. In a group interview, you attempt to interrupt, upstage or put down other candidates.

528. In a panel interview, you make eye contact more with certain people, and less with others.

529. The interviewer makes a comment that you take as insulting and you respond in kind.

530. You believe the interviewer is asking questions that are beneath your level of experience, so you say, "Can you ask me some better questions? These are far too basic for my level of experience".

531. You have tattoos and piercings and flaunt them.

532. You clasp your hands together in your lap and leave them there most of the time.

533. You wring your hands nervously, and are not even aware you do so.

534. When the interviewer tells you your answers are fairly short in length, you don't adjust.

535. When you ask the interviewer if they have any concerns about your candidacy, and they say no as they roll their eyes slightly, you don't follow up and probe.

536. As you search for the right word to say, you snap your fingers, drum the desk or scrunch your face up to signify how hard you are trying to remember.

537. During a panel interview you are distracted by some of the panelists speaking to each other as you answer.

538. The school told you not to bring a backpack, briefcase or binder to the interview, and you bring one of those.

539. When asked if you have any questions you pull out a folded up piece of paper from your pocket and begin reading from it.

540. You arrive dressed off-season. You wear short sleeves in winter and a long coat in summer.

541. You have plenty of enthusiasm, but it comes off as excess body energy, and you can't sit still.

542. You ask obvious questions that anyone can find on the company's website in two seconds.

543. As you are thinking, you look down at your feet, giving the impression that you are either ashamed, or low energy.

544. You bring items for "show and tell" without being asked.

545. You ask the interviewer if you can show them some samples of your work you brought with you and they decline, but you insist, and won't take no for an answer.

546. You have some of your work to show the interviewer on the web, but you forgot the URL.

547. You drop something you brought with you and get very upset or act very

seriously about it.

548. The interviewer makes an attempt to be humorous, and you miss it completely, and maintain a straight face.

549. You don't pay attention to time or number cues as part of the interviewer's questions. When they say take a minute or two to talk about x, you take five minutes, or a few seconds. When they say tell me two of your main strengths, you give them one, or five.

550. With each job requirement the interviewer describes you say, "I can do that...and that...and that", until you declare that there is nothing you can't do.

551. When the interviewer asks if there is any part of the job that you won't like, you say you "I like everything".

552. You use a new software program on your computer and can't operate it properly as part of your demonstration.

553. You prepare some questions, but not enough to last a series of interviews, or over the course of a few days, and you

run out.

554. You change the subject and take over the direction of the interview.

555. You ask questions that make the interviewer wonder if you trust him or really want to work there.

556. In an effort to appear smart, in the know, and eager, you finish the interviewer's questions.

557. The interviewer asks you to name three things you dislike about your previous boss and you comply, thinking you must answer what is asked of you.

558. Rather than talk about how you'll fit the job description, you just talk about yourself, and the interviewer pegs you as a narcissist.

559. You say you believe you are a good fit for the job and you say to the interviewer assumptively, "You think so too, don't you?"

560. Your answers are vague and never really precisely address the elements

contained in the question.

561. When asked by the interviewer to walk them through your resume, you really don't remember it very well, and you need to look at it.

562. You've been brought up to be polite, self-effacing and humble, so you are unable and unwilling to sell yourself.

563. You ask the interviewer if you can be interviewed by the person you'll be working for, instead of them.

564. You throw out some foreign language terms and say you speak it pretty well, and the interviewer happens to be fluent, and you get busted.

565. When asked about current events in your field, you really don't know what's going on in the news or in professional journals.

566. You are so relaxed the interviewer thinks you are either on drugs, or you really don't want the job and you are there simply practicing your interview skills.

567. You go on and on about how much you LOVE their company, thinking this ingratiation will get you hired.

568. When asked who your heroes in life are, you name the founders of the interviewer's company and give a book report about them.

569. Instead of using paraphrasing to display that you were listening to the question, you simply say, "I don't understand the question."

570. The interviewer's name is Tim and you call him Tom.

571. The interviewer's name is Thomas and you call him Tom.

572. In answer to the question "How are you different from our other candidates?", you give an answer that makes you a commodity, not something unique.

573. You don't vary and customize your answers to each company and each position.

574. At the interview, you inform the interviewer you need to leave early.

575. The interviewer asks what you believe is a trivial or unimportant question, and in answering it you clearly give it less enthusiasm or precision than other questions.

576. You come across to the interviewer as a complicated, emotional, full-of-drama person who is very unsettled and complex.

577. You say to the interviewer, "Convince me I should come to work here".

578. The interviewer is soft-spoken and you continue to talk loudly.

579. You present a list of "demands" or "must-haves" in the job.

" "

THE INTERVIEW GAME

"In most cases, the best strategy for a job interview is to be fairly honest, because the worst thing that can happen is that you won't get the job and will spend the rest of your life foraging for food in the wilderness and seeking shelter underneath a tree or the awning of a bowling alley that has gone out of business."

Lemony Snicket, Horseradish

"I always arrive late at the office, but I make up for it by leaving early."

Charles Lamb

"It's vital that you are sincere in an interview. Once you can fake that, you've got it made."

Bill Cole, MS, MA

53 MISTAKES YOU MAKE WITH BEHAVIORAL QUESTIONS

I know you can't WAIT to be asked a nice probing set of behavioral questions in an interview. You DREAM about these. Or maybe nightmare is a better word. Regardless, to know what you SHOULD do, you first have to know what you should NOT do. Here's that list.

1. When asked about a time you failed, and what you learned from it, you state that you have never failed at work.

2. The interviewer asks you a behavioral question, and you make up a situation.

3. You announce that you hate behavioral questions.

4. You ask not to be asked any behavioral questions.

5. You are asked a question where you have already used a fitting story for an earlier, different question, but you retell

the story, even though it doesn't fit this particular question.

6. After you tell a story, and the interviewer asks what you learned from that situation, you either say, "Nothing", or you can't come up with anything.

7. When describing how you work on a team, you are unclear about your role, and you either hog the credit or play down your leadership.

8. In answering the question "Tell me about a time you failed at something", you blame others, or circumstances or luck, instead of taking responsibility and then showing what you learned from the situation, and how you won't make that mistake again.

9. As you answer a behavioral question, the interviewer asks probing questions, and you are visibly irritated at being interrupted and being asked to go into more detail, other than your planned answer.

10. When the interviewer asks follow up questions and probing questions, you

believe they are bullying you.

11. You don't know how to identify and properly respond to "probing and challenging questions".

12. You don't know how to tell your best stories that highlight your strengths and capabilities.

13. You don't know how to make your stories dramatic, colorful and with good details of your strengths as they relate to the position you are seeking.

14. You don't know how to craft a representative set of stories about yourself that describe your good qualities, and then adapt, select and deliver each one to fit the questions asked in the actual interview.

15. You don't like telling stories, so you don't.

16. When the interviewer asks you a behavioral question, you give facts and data, not your experience in story form.

17. You believe that if the interviewer begins probing and asking follow up

questions, that means the interview has become hostile.

18. You don't recognize that behavioral interview technique questions begin with certain constructions such as "Please discuss...", "Take me through your thinking about..." and others.

19. When you select stories to tell, you choose very bland ones, or ones that don't highlight your strengths.

20. After a probing question, you place your arms across your chest, in a defensive posture.

21. You only have a few behavioral stories you can tell.

22. You think you can wing it and make up some stories on the spot.

23. When the interviewer begins to ask for details in your stories, you become upset, thinking they don't believe you.

24. When the interviewer asks the same thing over and over to your story, such as "So?", you get flustered and panic

for what to say.

25. The stories you tell are bare bones and too basic.

26. You tell stories that don't place you in a good light.

27. Your stories don't have a start, a middle and an end.

28. Your stories don't match what the interviewer is asking.

29. You choose stories that are good, but that happened far too long ago.

30. Your stories really don't wrap up logically, and instead, just drift off or fizzle out.

31. Your stories are disorganized and the interviewer has trouble following you.

32. You tell the same story twice, and try to adjust it to the new topic asked by the interviewer.

33. At the end of your stories, you rarely say, "What I learned from that

experience was...".

34. Your stories are far too short or far too long.

35. You give extraneous details in your stories that don't add any value.

36. You tell a good story, but at the end the interviewer says, "I don't see how that story answers my question".

37. The interviewer says, "Tell me about a time when you..." or "Describe a situation where you...", and you give facts and data, not a story.

38. The interviewer says, "Take me through your thinking about the XYZ project you did" and you don't describe your thinking at all, and just give a general description of your activities.

39. You don't have a story-telling formula such as S–Situation, A–Action, R–Result or P–Problem, A–Action, R–Result.

40. You display irritation when the interviewer interrupts you mid sentence to ask probing questions.

41. You have many stories, but not one about a so-called negative problem you overcame.

42. Your stories are from too many years ago and not suitable for business.

43. Your stories are bland because you have no conflict that needs to be resolved.

44. You make an excuse before you tell the story, saying it's not very good, but it's all you have.

45. You get sidetracked and go off on tangents.

46. You try to tell the story from memory, word for word.

47. Your story does not show that you're a better and stronger employee for the experience.

48. You tell a story that displays that you have bad character or poor integrity.

49. You tell a story that has political or religious overtones.

50. Your stories do not go beyond your resume bullet points.

51. Don't just recite a series of this happened, and then that happened sort of reporting style.

52. You tell too many stories in the same genre or theme.

53. You tell too many stories about your hobbies or personal life.

“ ”

THE INTERVIEW GAME

"In the name of all that is holy, please consider the wages of a particular profession before you select that degree plan."

**Miles Anthony Smith,
Becoming Generation Flux: Why
Traditional Career Planning is Dead**

"Besides getting several paper cuts in the same day or receiving the news that someone in your family has betrayed you to your enemies, one of the most unpleasant experiences in life is a job interview."

**Lemony Snicket,
The Carnivorous Carnival**

"The phrases 'Oh, goody' and 'job interview' rarely are heard together."

Bill Cole, MS, MA

25 MISTAKES YOU MAKE AS THE INTERVIEW ENDS

You only get one time to make a good first impression. You also only get one time to make a good LAST impression. This is known as bookending. You know, doing well at the start and finish. Leave the interviewer excited about your abilities and passion for their organization, and your life could change almost overnight. End the interview with a whimper and you'll wonder why you even showed up. Know this list of mistakes cold and you'll avoid needless self-inflicted damage.

1. At the end of the interview you ask, "How did I do?", "Do I have the job", "I got the job, right?", or "Am I better than the other applicants?"

2. You complete the interview and presumptively ask, "When do I start?" even though the interviewer has said nothing about you getting an offer.

3. The interviewer has clearly indicated that the interview has concluded, yet you press on by asking questions, or by saying, "I just wanted to clear up something that I said before."

4. At the end of the interview when they make you an offer, and you know you "have the job", you let your guard down and say things like, "I can't wait to get away from my psycho manager and that toxic company I'm with now!".

5. You get a job offer and ask the hiring manager to celebrate with you at a bar.

6. At the end of the interview, you ask, "So do I have the job?"

7. When the interviewer tells you that they will make you an offer, you let your guard down and relax to the point of acting like the interviewer is now your buddy.

8. In addition to the traditional handshake at the end of the interview, you attempt to hug the interviewer.

9. After completing the interview you enter the company bathroom, change out of your suit and tie, walk through the lobby, and leave.

10. After the interviewer signals that the interview is over, you quickly stand up and leave the room.

11. The interview goes very well, and you believe you may have the job, (or the interviewer says that or hints at that) and you let down your guard and begin behaving too casually, giddily, or too presumptively.

12. After the interview, you are in a hurry to leave the room.

13. You don't know how to artfully end the interview, and when to linger and when to leave.

14. You don't know how to close the interview with a unique statement that makes you memorable.

15. You don't know what to do and say after the interview is over, and how to follow up.

16. You don't know strategies on salary and contract negotiation so you get the best possible financial package.

17. You see the interviewer wrapping up to conclude, or to leave the room, yet you just sit there and don't gather your things.

18.	You don't make a final statement, and instead just let the interview slow down into a typical bland conclusion.

19.	You don't shake hands when you leave the room.

20.	You don't thank the interviewer for their time, at a minimum.

21.	You don't know how to behave before and after "the official, live interview", while you are walking or waiting with the interviewer.

22.	You get up to leave before the interviewer does.

23.	You walk out of the interview, and you are observed removing your tie or sport coat as soon as you are outside the building, as you walk away.

24.	At the end of the interview you shake the interviewer's hand using both of yours.

25.	When walking out of the interview you pat the interviewer on their arm or shoulder or back.

" **"**

THE INTERVIEW GAME

"I get mad at people who talk about traumatic
job interviews, about going on one and
getting rejected. I get rejected all the time
and not only do I get rejected,
but people have no problem being
really specific about why I was rejected."

Julia Sweeney, SNL star

"Trying is the first step towards failure."

Homer Simpson

"You have to go into your interview thinking
how lucky this company will be to get you."

Bill Cole, MS, MA

54 MISTAKES YOU MAKE FOLLOWING UP AFTER THE INTERVIEW

Many people make a BIG mistake after their interview. They don't follow up at all! This is not the time to let up and go on cruise control. You need to keep the pedal to the metal and keep that intensity flowing until the offer comes in, and even longer, until you SIGN that offer. Lots of bad things can happen in this phase, and you want to avoid every one of them. So fasten your seatbelt and keep your arms inside the ride at all times.

1. After the interview you send an email to the interviewer apologizing for your poor performance in the interview, asking to still be considered for the position.

2. In your list of references you provide outdated or incorrect phone numbers to force the interviewer to do research to find the correct number.

3. You are clearly in a hurry to leave.

4.   You rebuff the interviewer's desire for more small talk in a desire to continue "selling yourself'.

5.   You get on your cell phone while still in the room, hallway or lobby.

6.   You fail to send a timely thank you note, or even one at all.

7.   You fail to follow up with the company, even if they said to wait, and they then assume you are not assertive enough.

8.   You post the questions asked in your interview on social media, and the company finds out.

9.   You don't immediately leave the company premises and can be seen walking around for some time.

10. You contact people other than the interviewer to inquire what they thought of you in the interview.

11. You hang out in the lobby for no apparent reason.

12. You sit in your car in the company parking lot and eat lunch.

13. You blast music from your car in the company parking lot.

14. The person you invited to either pick you up or meet you at the lobby is less than presentable.

15. If you were interviewed by multiple people, you address one note to "Dear All" instead of writing individual notes to all those with whom you had an official interaction.

16. You ask the interviewer if you can "bum a cigarette".

17. You become too familiar after an interview, and in emails use Hey, instead of Hi, or Hello.

18. As you walk out the door of the company you immediately light up a cigarette.

19. You send the interviewer a gift after the interview.

20.   You make far too many calls and emails to follow up.

21.   You tell the interviewer that your friend will be unable to give you a ride home, and ask if they can take you.

22.   You continually email the interviewer, asking what else you can do to advance your candidacy.

23.   You send the interviewer a request to join you on LinkedIn or Facebook.

24.   You show up at the interviewer's office randomly "to check in".

25.   You send a text message instead of a thank you note that says, "thx 4 mtg".

26.   You receive a call or email from the recruiter or interviewer that the position was filled by someone else, and you proceed to attempt to convince them that they made the wrong decision, and that they should really reconsider you more closely.

27.   You become irritated at how long it takes for the interviewer to get back to you after the interview, so to retaliate,

you take your time responding when they finally contact you for additional data for your application.

28. Upon learning from the interviewer that you did not get the job, you let them know how unhappy you are about that, treat them disrespectfully and trash their company.

29. You don't trade business cards with your interviewer, so it's hard to follow up.

30. You send so many emails and make so many calls that it is obvious you would need extreme hand-holding, and be very needy once on the job.

31. You have careless typos in your written correspondence.

32. You leave a voicemail for the interviewer, leaving off your last name or other identifying details, so they are not sure it's really you or not.

33. You become very friendly and have a familiar tone with the interviewer, as if you are now buddies.

34. You negotiate so long and so hard on salary and package that the interviewer gets second thoughts about you.

35. You have non-professional email, twitter and other social media names.

36. You send your resume and other items as word docs (instead as a PDF) and when the interviewer opens them, their email system corrupts the formatting, making them look horrible.

37. If you've not heard back from the interviewer, you send an angry email or leave a voicemail saying, "Why haven't you called me back?"

38. In salary negotiations, you state the first set of numbers, and lose the advantage.

39. In your thank you note, you simply re-list your qualifications and experience.

40. In your thank you note, you mismatch the tone of the organization and the interviewer. If it was a casual, friendly interview, you make the note formal and officious. If it was a more serious interview, you make the note frivolous

and glib.

41. In your thank you note, you write a novel or recount your life's story.

42. In your thank you note, if your skill set or experience is not perfect for the position, don't apologize for that.

43. You have typos or crossed-out words in your written thank you note.

44. In your thank you note, you sound desperate by being extra friendly, too personal, begging-sounding or gratuitous.

45. In your thank you note, you use a non-professional writing style and say you'd LOVE to work there, or that this is your DREAM job.

46. In your thank you note, you apologize for something that happened in the interview.

47. In your thank you note you ask about salary or benefits or special contract items.

48. In your thank you note, you give bland, trite or generic compliments about the organization or the interviewer.

49. In your thank you note, you ask for a referral for a different position or a different company.

50. In your thank you note, you ask for a favor or for special treatment.

51. You don't know the best ways to write thank you letters and emails.

52. You don't know how to review your interviews to discover what went well, and what still needs to be improved.

53. After a job offer, you ask the interviewer to postpone the start date so you could still get holiday gifts from vendors at your current job.

54. You don't know ways to "stay in touch" with the interviewer, so you show your continued interest, and so you stay "top of mind" without being seen as a pest.

" **"**

THE INTERVIEW GAME

"I didn't have a job because nobody would
hire me. My friends were getting hired, and I
couldn't even get a job interview.
That really rocked my self-esteem because
I didn't understand what I did wrong
on those job applications."
Tyra Banks

"I picked up an issue of Cosmopolitan the
other day that had tips for job interviews,
because I was like, 'I need to get better at
interviews.' The article was basically about
how to get someone not to hate you in 20
minutes."
Jennifer Lawrence

"All job hunters need mental toughness and
resillence. Or good medication."
Bill Cole, MS, MA

81 INTERVIEW MISTAKES MADE BY PEOPLE OVER 50

There is a special art to interviewing for folks over the age of 50. There are special hurdles to overcome. These obstacles exist mainly in the mind of the interviewers who have many biases and preconceived notions of older people. But there are also subtle adjustments and a change in mindset required from the older interviewee. I don't like sounding like Mr. Doom and Gloom, but it's good to be realistic. Positive thinking is key. But I had one client, when I asked if he was a positive thinker who said, "Yes. I am. I'm positive I won't get the job I want". THAT is not positive thinking.

1.   You state that you have over 30 years experience, and use other such cumulative experience resume state-ments on your resume.

2.   You are not ready to discuss the interviewer's concerns about how you stayed at one company for 20 years. This makes them think you aren't nimble and change-capable.

3.   You don't even consider using either over the counter or dentist-provided

teeth whitening procedures.

4.   You write a chronological resume instead of a functional resume one that hides your age.

5.   You are too honest and talk about some aches and pains you have, and some health issues.

6.   You don't interview with firms that value older workers and who have an older demographic in their customers.

7.   You are not up to date with the current trends and technologies in your field.

8.   You don't display a sense of humor. This makes you look stodgy, boring and tired.

9.   You show the interviewer how "wise you are".

10. You show disrespect to the interviewer because you were hoping for someone older.

11. You believe the interviewer will immediately value your years of experience, and that you will barely

have to sell yourself.

12.   You display your decades of experience by dominating the conversation.

13.   You dress "too young".

14.   You talk "too young".

15.   You act "too young".

16.   You say you have a child the interviewer's age in an effort to build rapport.

17.   Your voice mail greeting says, "Please leave a message...for my Grampa", voiced by your granddaughter.

18.   When asked what you do for fun, you say you just completed cataloguing your LP record collection, and went to a film festival for 1950's musicals.

19.   You assume the younger interviewer is not the boss, and they can sense it.

20.   You say your years of experience and trial and error have taught you the "best ways to work", thereby making

you sound set in your ways.

21. You say your resume or experience speaks for itself. You will come across as entitled.

22. You tell stories or use examples that are old instead of keeping them current.

23. You use cultural references that are too old. No one knows who Bob Hope is any more.

24. You say, "In my day...". the interviewer will think, "So THIS isn't your day, huh?"

25. You say you could be "the house mother or father" to the team.

26. You either don't have a LinkedIn profile or it's barren.

27. You pull out a day planner or calendar.

28. You complain that cell phone text size is hard to read.

29.   You don't text. You don't like it.

30.   You don't even know what Twitter, Skype and Facetime is.

31.   You say you only use email on your computer because it's easier to read and type.

32.   You pull out an ancient flip phone.

33.   You complain about Facebook, and social media.

34.   You say you "just don't understand" the social media craze.

35.   You use an old photo that makes you look aged.

36.   You are seen reading or discussing a newspaper. That something older people do. Younger people get their news on line.

37.   Your voicemail greeting sounds stodgy, picky and boring.

38.   You don't color your hair to soften some of the gray.

39. You wear a black suit. Black can have a "too serious look" and remind people of funerals and people in authority. Black can potentially make you look stuffy and too conservative in your thinking.

40. You are out of shape and that makes it all too easy for the interviewer to decide you won't be energetic or have staying power and vitality day to day.

41. You use an old-style format for your resume.

42. You go back too far on your job chronology on your resume. 10-15 years is standard.

43. You are so knowledgeable about the field that you actually correct the interviewer on some errors.

44. You say you can be a mentor to the interviewer.

45. You say you are 55 years OLD. Instead, say you are 55 years OF AGE. Or say you are 55 years YOUNG.

46. You say "This is before your time but..."

47. The interviewer shares a challenge of theirs about work and you say, "That used to be a problem for me too at your age".

48. You think (or even say) that being qualified, working hard, and being loyal to a company is enough to get you a job.

49. You have heard the new concept called "Interviewing Younger" about being perceived as more youthful at work by altering your word choice, body language, and look, but you refuse to believe it.

50. You mention your adult children, your grandchildren and...even your GREAT grandchildren.

51. You whip out pictures of your grandkids doing cute things.

52. You use cultural terms that were popular in the 70's, 80's and 90's.

53. You don't have your email address on your resume.

54. You have an email address with Aol.com, earthlink or netzero.com indicating you got it ages ago and never upgraded.

55. When asked what social media sites you frequent, you say "Huh"?

56. You constantly repeat various buzz words and phrases to the interviewer you believe are "hip and youthful sounding".

57. You refer to a new piece of technology as "new-fangled".

58. You say, "It's good for a dinosaur like me to be around young, vibrant people. You'll keep me young".

59. The interviewer shows you a new app on their phone and you say incredulously, "What won't they think of next?!"

60. You act self-conscious and insecure about your age as you say, "Anyone my age around here?", or "Pretty young team, huh?"

61. You describe everything you have done so far, and very little of what you will do next for the company.

62. You puff up the job titles on your resume to look important, but the interviewer sees you as overqualified.

63. When asked about your plans for the next five years and beyond, you mention retirement and slowing down.

64. You mention that your wife is retired, and you both look forward to a time when things "are not so hectic".

65. You say that one of your great joys in life is playing with the grandkids.

66. You say you won't need much guidance, since you are so experienced, and the interviewer thinks, "So he won't take direction well".

67. The interviewer's business is young, fast-paced and edgy, and when asked if you have any hobbies, you describe your stamp collection, your love of flea markets and how often you go on cruises, mainly for the buffets.

68. When asked to read a document, you fumble for your glasses, muttering, "I really need to get my prescription checked soon. My eyes seem to be getting worse and worse".

69. You say, "I've done this job before, so you will never have to tell me what to do", and the interviewer hears a big ego know-it-all.

70. You say you are ready for a change, that your current company just does not excite you anymore.

71. You are overly enthusiastic about some new technology or social media, and describe it incorrectly or use wrong terminology with it.

72. You say you could see yourself staying in this job until you retire, thinking your loyalty will be admired.

73. You say that with your years of experience, you can help this company avoid many pitfalls, traps and bad decisions, because you're "been there, done that".

74. You mainly talk about what you've DONE and not very much about what

you want TO DO.

75. You act formal and "corporate", with impeccable manners, yet you come across as stiff, lifeless and...old.

76. You are clueless about words or phrases that have acquired non-professional meanings, and use them in the interview.

77. You've worked with some real heavy weights in the business, but you name-drop people that are perceived as dinosaurs, or worse, as unrecognizable.

78. You talk about your recent 24th wedding anniversary celebration, and other life events that mark you as old.

79. You have a three or four page CV because you want to show how experienced you are.

80. You indicate indirectly that "You've paid your dues" and that you expect to start at a higher level than younger people, and also to be able to avoid much of the "grunt work", since you've "earned that right".

81. When asked about the current business climate, and your predictions about the future, you lament, "It's not like the good old days!"

THE INTERVIEW GAME

"Desire! That's the one secret of every man's career. Not education. Not being born with hidden talents. Desire."

Bobby Unser, three-time Indianapolis 500 winner

"I sometimes find that in interviews you learn more about yourself than the person learned about you."

William Shatner

"In most sales situations people buy on emotion, and justify their purchase on logic, and interviewing is no different, so make sure you sell yourself using passion and enthusiasm."

Bill Cole, MS, MA

104 ULTIMATE SELF-SABOTAGING INTERVIEW MISTAKES

I know. I know. You're wondering if I've contacted the Guinness Book Of World Records people about these "special mistakes". Not yet. But I might. These 104 mistakes are certainly worthy of close inspection, because these are killers. These are the rattlesnakes of the interview world. Step on one of these babies and you're likely to get tossed out the door. Read this chapter at your own risk. And I hope you've had all your shots.

1.   You tell the interviewer, "Can you sign this paper for me stating I was here looking for a job? It's for my parole officer and I have to make a stab at getting back into society."

2.   You tell the interviewer, "Can we reschedule the follow-up interview? I have an appointment at the tattoo parlor on that day."

3.   You tell the interviewer, when one applicant was asked, "What person would you like to have dinner with,

living or dead?" he replied, "The living one."

4. You tell the interviewer, "My friends at the bar said this might be a nice place to work because it's so close and all."

5. You tell the interviewer, "How many times can I be late to work before I get fired?"

6. You tell the interviewer, "My last boss tried to send me to Anger Management Class and that really ticked me off."

7. You tell the interviewer, "I'm Wiccan. Can I get all the equinoxes and solstices off?"

8. You tell the interviewer, "One of my accomplishments? Well, I was never convicted."

9. You tell the interviewer, "One of my strengths? "I work well with a hangover, which is a something not many people can do."

10. You tell the interviewer, "When would the first paycheck be coming out?"

11. You tell the interviewer, "This won't take too long, will it? I have another interview lined up."

12. You tell the interviewer, "Regarding question 12 here where it says "Felonies". You just mean "convicted" ...right?"

13. You send your resume to the office crumpled up inside of a shoe. The note said, "Just trying to get my foot in the door."

14. When the interviewer asked, "What is your greatest accomplishment?" you replied, "Writing my first novel." When the interviewer said, "I mean something you have accomplished in a work setting." You say, "Well, actually I wrote most of it while at work!"

15. You mention that you are crossing the state line to attend the interview, and that is in violation of your probation, but that you feel the interview was worth risking the possible jail time.

16. When the interviewer tells you they'll not be able to offer you a job because, even if you qualified for the position, your drug test came back positive, and

this was a drug/alcohol-free environment. You then ask, 'Can you tell me
which one showed up on the test
results?'"

17.   You have rings on almost every finger,
and as you talk with your hands they
go 'Clink, clank, clack'.

18.   You begin the interview by asking the
interviewer, "So, tell me about
yourself".

19.   You attempt to convert the interviewer
to your religion.

20.   When asked, "Why should I hire you?",
you say, "I'm good looking, how can
you not hire me?"

21.   You bring urine to an interview thinking
you might have to take a drug test.

22.   You arrive in a jogging suit because you
want to go running after the interview.

23.   You stop in the restroom just before
your interview. You share with a
woman there whom you don't know
that you feel you will have to fake the
interview because you're not qualified

and this person turns out to be the interviewer.

24. You bring a "how to interview" book with you to the interview and consult it as you go.

25. You brag about how prompt you are, yet you show up 10 minutes late.

26. You ask the interviewer, "What company is this again?"

27. You bring in a sport trophy you won to show the interviewer to prove you're a hard worker.

28. You ask the interviewer's admin out on a date.

29. The first thing you say in the interview is, "I just want you to know that I can't be hired for less than "X" amount of dollars. I think you should know that first of all".

30. You tell the interviewer that you were let go from your previous job because the boss was threatened by your intelligence and they were afraid you were going to take their job.

31. You arrive for a job at Starbucks holding a coffee from Pete's Coffee shop, or some other competitor.

32. When you interviewed for a bartending job, when asked to describe your experience as a bartender, you said that you were very good at drinking so that is why you could be a good bartender.

33. When discussing schedules, you say that you don't like to be tied down to a schedule and find it too constricting to have to be at a certain place at a certain time.

34. The receptionist asks you if you would like a piece of candy. You take the basket and proceed to take handfuls and stuff them in your pockets.

35. When asked if you have a reliable source of transportation, you say, "Well my mom would be driving me, and she's pretty reliable".

36. You show up unannounced and ask to be interviewed then and there because you were "in the area".

37. You ask the interviewer to pay for the taxi you took to get to the interview.

38. After the company declines you for a job, you repeatedly call and email, demanding to know how someone could be better qualified than you were.

39. You use buzzwords that you obviously don't understand.

40. After being asked a particularly tough question, you stop the interviewer, and ask if you can dial your therapist.

41. In the lobby you help yourself to an apple from the office fruit bowl while waiting to be called in. You take a bite and find it isn't to your taste, so you simply put the marred fruit back into the bowl.

42. You are rushing to park your car in time for your interview. Temporarily stuck behind another vehicle in the garage, you angrily flip the driver the bird. When the driver ignores you, you begin honking your horn and shouting insults. And when you finally manage to park, you run upstairs to the interview room, only to come face-to-face with...the driver of the other car.

43. You try to use foreign language words and phrases to impress the interviewer, but you do so in a very bad accent.

44. You tell the interviewer that you see the company has various sports leagues and you brag about how you could help them win championships.

45. You ask the interviewer for some cash so you can buy a sandwich on the way home.

46. When asked why you want this position, you answer, "My horoscope tells me this would be a good move".

47. When asked about your strengths, you give an answer that involves only social or recreational attributes.

48. When asked if you have been convicted of a crime, you state, "No. But I came real close a few times".

49. When asked to describe your weak-nesses, you state, "I hate these types of questions".

50. You state, "I hope I do OK at this interview. I'm still hung over from last

night".

51. When asked to describe a time you made a mistake on the job, and how you dealt with it, you say, "I stole something, but they let me pay the company back and resign instead of calling the cops".

52. When asked why you left your last job, you state, "It was better than staying there. One more day and I would have killed my boss".

53. When asked why they should hire you, you give a reason having nothing to do with their business. For example, you say, "The schedule here fits perfectly with my golf schedule".

54. When asked what your weaknesses are, you say, "I have an anger problem, but as long as I stay on my meds, I am usually OK".

55. When asked if you have given two weeks notice at your current job, you answer, "Oh, if I get this job here, I'll tell those jerks off and leave the same day".

56. When asked why you chose this organization, you reply, "My mother thought it could be a good stepping stone".

57. When asked what your ideal job would be, you answer glibly, "A drug dealer. The money is huge, and you barely have to work".

58. You ask the interviewer if you can take a five-minute break to check your email, or you just start checking it.

59. You ask the interviewer, "If I get an offer, can I wait three weeks before I have to take the drug test?"

60. You ask the interviewer, "Do you actually work here, or are you an outside temp agency worker?"

61. When asked, "How are you?", you state, "Much better. My rehab ended last week and I feel free again".

62. You tell the interviewer that you "took a tranquilizer for nerves today" and that the interview was not truly indicative of your real personality.

63. You ask questions like "What is your drug-testing policy?", or "I'm worried about the background checks. Do you guys do background checks?", or "Does being arrested, but not convicted count as having a criminal background?"

64. When asked about why you left your previous job, you state that you can't say much because you are still in litigation with them.

65. You ask, "I traveled many miles to get here, so who do I ask about expense reimbursement?"

66. You ask things that make the interviewer suspicious such as, "Do you require a physician's note when I take a sick day" or "How soon can I take a sick day or personal day off?"

67. When asked what you know about the position, you say, "I hear the pay is good", or "My friend said the benefits rock", or "The job looks pretty easy".

68. You ask if the company conducts background checks, and how important those are.

69. When asked why you left your last job you say that everyone was out to get you.

70. You ask if you need to pass a drug test and how much advance notice is given.

71. You disclose, without being asked, that you are a recovering drug addict or alcoholic, but that you are "clean now".

72. You disclose, without being asked, that you have spent extensive time in psychotherapy.

73. You disclose, without being asked, that you were fired from a job.

74. You disclose, without being asked, your religious affiliations.

75. You disclose, without being asked, details of your divorce or love life.

76. You disclose, without being asked, that you have certain medical issues, but that they won't hamper your ability to perform the job.

77. You disclose, without being asked, that you have a history of being the victim

of crime.

78. You disclose, without being asked, that you have had lots of bad luck in your life.

79. You disclose, without being asked, that you are accident-prone.

80. You disclose, without being asked, that you sued a former employer.

81. You disclose, without being asked, that you have been in court often for various reasons.

82. You disclose, without being asked, that you assaulted a former employer.

83. You disclose, without being asked, about recent deaths or tragedies in your life.

84. You disclose, without being asked, that you are hoping to start your own business soon.

85. You disclose, without being asked, that you are hoping to learn enough from this job to start your own, similar business.

86.	You disclose, without being asked, that you are hoping this will be the last job you ever need to have.

87.	You disclose, without being asked, that you need this job so you can make the rent, pay off a car loan, get things out of hock, or keep someone off your back, to whom you owe money.

88.	You disclose, without being asked, that you are very nervous.

89.	You disclose, without being asked, that you are not very interested in their company, but you need a job.

90.	You ask if there are cameras watching you as you work.

91.	You ask if the company will monitor your Internet and email use while at work.

92.	In an effort to be clever, on the application where it asks for an "Emergency Contact" you write, "Call 911".

93.	You arrange to have fast food delivered right into the interview room.

94. In an effort to be funny, on the application where it asks for "Salary Desired" you write, "of course".

95. In an effort to be funny, you refer to the young staff or team of the interviewer as "kids", "young-uns", "teenie-boppers" or "the JV team".

96. You bring free movie passes or gift certificates with you to the interview and attempt to give them to the interviewer as a bribe.

97. You bring a pet of any kind with you.

98. You call in sick to your current employer during the interview, faking an illness.

99. When you are asked the question on the application "Have you ever been convicted of a felony", you respond, "I'm not sure. I'll know next month".

100. You put down a certain class of people, or type of profession.

101. You bring a child, dog or other animal with you.

102. You place a good luck charm you brought on the interviewer's desk.

103. You ask to change chairs or rooms because where the interviewer wants you to sit is considered "bad Feng Shui".

104. You bring a gift to the interviewer.

BILL COLE, MS, MA

Bill Cole, MS, MA is a nationally-recognized media personality and interview coach and the author of 17 books on interview skills, including the well-selling book, *The Interview Success Guide* and the book *Interview Mistakes You Don't Even Know You're Making.*

Bill is regularly interviewed by the media on interviewing strategies by such career outlets as Monster.com, LEADx.org, Riley Guide Careers Blog, Business Insider magazine, Dice magazine, SimplyHired.com and Yahoo Style Magazine.

Bill is an expert at coaching people on how to shine in media and business interviews. He developed this skill set over decades of being involved with the media—on the inside—and on the outside. Countless times, Bill has either been interviewed by the media himself and/or coached people to give successful interviews with them. You no doubt recognize these big media outlets where Bill's work has appeared, and/or where he has helped his clients get press attention:

MSNBC.com, Golf Magazine, the BBC, ABC-TV, Fox News, the Associated Press Radio, Sirius Radio, The New York Times, Success Magazine, The Washington Post, Corporate & Incentive Travel magazine, The San Francisco Examiner and Chronicle, Yahoo! Sports, ABC-TV, Entrepreneur Magazine, The San Jose Mercury News, The Denver Post, The Detroit News, The Buffalo News, The Kansas City Star, Tennis Magazine, Runner's World, Fitness Magazine, Presentations Magazine, Professionally Speaking, Time Magazine, the Los Angeles Times and USA Today. There are many others.

For years, Bill has improved thousands of people's interview skills to help them advance in their careers, enter professional, graduate and medical schools and shine in media interviews on TV and radio.

Bill has trained people in better interview and career-strategies in high tech, the executive suite, engineering, sales, finance, consulting, customer service, education, politics, government, medical school, osteopathic school, dental school, pharmacy school, chiropractic school, physical therapy school, nursing school, and all other allied health care field interviews. He has taught people state of the art interviewing skills to foreign dentists and physicians wishing to begin US practices, physicians seeking residency programs and fellowships, psychiatrists, psychologists, MFT's, LCSW's, therapists, counselors, police, law enforcement, civil service, and law firms.

There is a counseling and career coaching perspective to Bill's work as an interview coach that few other interview coaches possess. He was a psychotherapist at one time and holds a master's degree in Counseling Psychology. Bill regularly helps his clients "figure out who they are" and what their values, goals and dreams are so they can portray themselves authentically in their interviews and match themselves precisely to the position or school they are seeking.

"Bill Cole is a leading Olympic sports psychologist and a world-renowned peak performance coach."

**British Broadcasting Corporation
(The BBC)**

"Bill Cole is a world-leading authority
on sports psychology."

**New Idea Magazine,
Coleman-Rayner, LLC**

"Bill Cole is a leading author
on sports psychology."

Yahoo! Sports

"Bill Cole is a renowned sports psychologist
and 'mental game coach' who helps
athletes cope with the demands
of intense competition."

CNET Magazine

Index

www.ingramcontent.com/pod-product-compliance
Lightning Source LLC
Chambersburg PA
CBHW060245100426

42742CB00011B/1649